Kim Hargreaves
Vintage Designs to Knit

Kim Hargreaves
Vintage Designs to Knit

25 Timeless Patterns for Women and Men
from the Rowan Collection

Edited by KATE BULLER

TS

TRAFALGAR SQUARE
North Pomfret, Vermont

Kim Hargreaves: Vintage Designs to Knit
First published in the United States of America in 2011
By Trafalgar Square Books
North Pomfret, Vermont 05053

Created and produced by Berry & Bridges Ltd
Suite 416, Belsize Business Centre
258 Belsize Road
London NW6 4BT

Editor: Katie Hardwicke
Technical editor: Sue Whiting
Designer: Nicky Downes, Downes Design

ISBN 978 1 57076 494 3

Library of Congress Number: 2011929195

Reproduced and printed in Singapore

Contents

Introduction

Kim's design career with Rowan stretches back to 1987 when Stephen Sheard, the founder of Rowan, encouraged her to create her first knitwear design for *The Cotton Collection*. Her mother, Kathleen, had been running the Design Room at Rowan for several years before that, and Kim's very first experience at Rowan was as a teenager, when she helped her mother out during the school break.

Kim's natural eye for shape, texture, and color quickly became obvious, but she was already steeped in the tradition of needlecraft as a child. Kim quickly built on her initial success and gradually extended her role to oversee the photography shoots for the Rowan magazine and many brochures, and helping to select new yarns and colors, as she became Rowan's head in-house designer.

What makes Kim's talent so special is that her designs incorporate that rare thing in knitwear design—a clear sense of style with a real love and knowledge of the actual craft of handknitting. Her designs have cross-generational appeal and, perhaps even more important, they stand the test of time. Looking through the patterns in this book, you would find it hard to know exactly when they were designed—the real hallmark of a classic.

In recent years, Kim has set up her own label "Kim" but still works with Rowan yarns, although now she has a palette of her own shades in some of her favorite yarns. Those wanting to know more about her current work can visit her website, www.kimhargreaves.co.uk. If you want to know more about the yarns used in this book or the current shades available, visit the Rowan website, www.knitrowan.com.

A few of the yarns Kim used for the designs in this book are no longer available, although we have tried to pick our classic yarns where possible. Substitutes with similar gauge from the current Rowan shadecards are suggested, although particular care needs to be taken to get the gauge in the pattern correct.

We hope you enjoy revisiting these, some of our favorite designs by Kim, and that a new generation of Rowan knitters finds them equally appealing.

Kate Buller
Senior Brand Manager, Rowan Yarns

Audrey

This retro 50s style boat-neck cotton sweater, knitted in Rowan *Calmer*, makes a great summer knit, teamed with cropped pants or a flowery skirt. The neatly fitted top is knitted in a wide rib to give it a figure-hugging quality, and the neck is finished off with a neat, but simple, lacy edging. It would not be too difficult for a relatively inexperienced knitter. If Coral is not your color, there are plenty of other soft but bright summery colors in this yarn.

YARN AND SIZES

	XS	S	M	L	XL	
To fit bust	32	34	36	38	40	in
	81	86	91	97	102	cm

Aran (CYCA Medium) yarn
Rowan *Calmer* (75% cotton, 25% acrylic microfiber; 175yd/50g) in Coral 476

	6	7	7	7	8	balls

NEEDLES
1 pair size 7 (4.5mm) needles
1 pair size 8 (5mm) needles

GAUGE
21 sts and 30 rows to 4in/10cm measured over stockinette stitch using size 8 (5mm) needles *or size necessary to obtain correct gauge.*

BACK and FRONT (both alike)

Cast on 90 (96: 102: 108: 114) sts using 4.5mm (US 7) needles.

Row 1 (RS): K0 (1: 0: 1: 0), *P2, K2, rep from * to last 2 (3: 2: 3: 2) sts, P2, K0 (1: 0: 1: 0).

Row 2: P0 (1: 0: 1: 0), *K2, P2, rep from * to last 2 (3: 2: 3: 2) sts, K2, P0 (1: 0: 1: 0).

These 2 rows form rib.

Work in rib for a further 4 rows, ending with a WS row.

Change to size 8 (5mm) needles.

Work in rib for a further 4 rows, ending with a WS row.

Place marker on 25th (26th: 29th: 30th: 33rd) st in from both ends of last row.

Next row (RS): Rib to within 3 sts of marked st, K3tog, P marked st, rib to next marked st, P marked st, K3tog tbl, rib to end.

Work 7 rows.

Rep last 8 rows twice more, then first of these rows (the dec row) again. *74 (80: 86: 92: 98) sts.*

Work 9 rows, ending with a WS row.

Next row (RS): Rib to marked st, M1, P marked st, rib to next marked st, P marked st, M1, rib to end.

Work 5 rows.

Rep last 6 rows 6 times more, then first of these rows (the inc row) again, taking inc sts into rib. *90 (96: 102: 108: 114) sts.*

Cont even until work measures 13 (13¹/₂: 13¹/₂: 13³/₄: 13³/₄)in/33 (34: 34: 35: 35)cm, ending with a WS row.

Shape armholes

Keeping rib correct, bind off 5 sts at beg of next 2 rows. *80 (86: 92: 98: 104) sts.*

Next row (RS): P2, K2, P1, P2tog, rib to last 7 sts, P2tog tbl, P1, K2, P2.

Next row: K2, P2, K1, K2tog tbl, rib to last 7 sts, K2tog, K1, P2, K2.

Rep last 2 rows 0 (0: 1: 1: 2) times more. *76 (82: 84: 90: 92) sts.*

Next row (RS): P2, K2, P1, P2tog, rib to last 7 sts, P2tog tbl, P1, K2, P2.

Next row: K2, P2, K2, rib to last 6 sts, K2, P2, K2.

Rep last 2 rows 4 (5: 6: 7: 8) times more. *66 (70: 70: 74: 74) sts.*

Work a further 22 (20: 20: 18: 16) rows, ending with a WS row.

Bind off in rib.

SLEEVES (both alike)

Cast on 56 (56: 58: 60: 60) sts using size 7 (4.5mm) needles.

Row 1 (RS): P0 (0: 0: 1: 1), K1 (1: 2: 2: 2), *P2, K2, rep from * to last 3 (3: 0: 1: 1) sts, P2 (2: 0: 1: 1), K1 (1: 0: 0: 0).

Row 2: K0 (0: 0: 1: 1), P1 (1: 2: 2: 2), *K2, P2, rep from * to last 3 (3: 0: 1: 1) sts, K2 (2: 0: 1: 1), P1 (1: 0: 0: 0).

These 2 rows form rib.

Work in rib for a further 4 rows, ending with a WS row.

Change to size 8 (5mm) needles.

Cont in rib, shaping sides by inc 1 st at each end of 15th and every foll 14th (14th: 14th: 14th: 12th) row to 68 (68: 62: 76: 70) sts, then on every foll 12th (12th: 12th: -: 10th) row until there are 72 (72: 76: -: 80) sts, taking inc sts into rib.

Cont even until sleeve measures 17 (17: 17¹/₂: 17¹/₂: 17¹/₂)in/43 (43: 44: 44: 44)cm, ending with a WS row.

Shape top

Keeping rib correct, bind off 5 sts at beg of next 2 rows. *62 (62: 66: 66: 70) sts.*

Next row (RS): P2, K2, P1, P2tog, rib to last 7 sts, P2tog tbl, P1, K2, P2.

Next row: K2, P2, K1, K2tog tbl, rib to last 7 sts, K2tog, K1, P2, K2. *58 (58: 62: 62: 66) sts.*

Next row (RS): P2, K2, P1, P2tog, rib to last 7 sts, P2tog tbl, P1, K2, P2.

Next row: K2, P2, K2, rib to last 6 sts, K2, P2, K2.

Rep last 2 rows 2 (2: 4: 4: 7) times more. *52 (52: 52: 52: 50) sts.*

Next row (RS): P2, K2, P1, P2tog, rib to last 7 sts, P2tog tbl, P1, K2, P2.

Next row: K2, P2, K2, rib to last 6 sts, K2, P2, K2.
Next row: P2, K2, P2, rib to last 6 sts, P2, K2, P2.
Next row: K2, P2, K2, rib to last 6 sts, K2, P2, K2.
Rep last 4 rows 5 (5: 5: 5: 4) times more, then first 2 of these rows again.
Bind off rem 38 sts.

FINISHING
PRESS as described on the information page 138.
Join raglan seams using back stitch, or mattress stitch if preferred.
Neck edging
Cast on 12 sts using size 7 (4.5mm) needles.
Row 1 and every foll alt row: K1, yo, P2tog, K to end.
Row 2: K2, yo, K3, yo, skp, K2, yo, P2tog, K1. *13 sts.*
Row 4: K2, yo, K5, yo, skp, K1, yo, P2tog, K1. *14 sts.*
Row 6: K2, yo, K3, yo,skp, K2, yo, skp, yo, P2tog, K1. *15 sts.*
Row 8: K1, K2tog, yo, skp, K3, K2tog, yo, K2, yo, P2tog, K1. *14 sts.*
Row 10: K1, K2tog, yo, skp, K1, K2tog, yo, K3, yo, P2tog, K1. *13 sts.*
Row 12: K1, K2tog, yo, sk2p, yo, K4, yo, P2tog, K1. *12 sts.*
Rep these 12 rows until neck edging, when slightly stretched, fits around entire neck edge, ending with row 12.
Bind off.
Join ends of neck edging, then sew straight edge to neck edge, placing seam level with left back armhole seam. See information page 138 for finishing instructions.

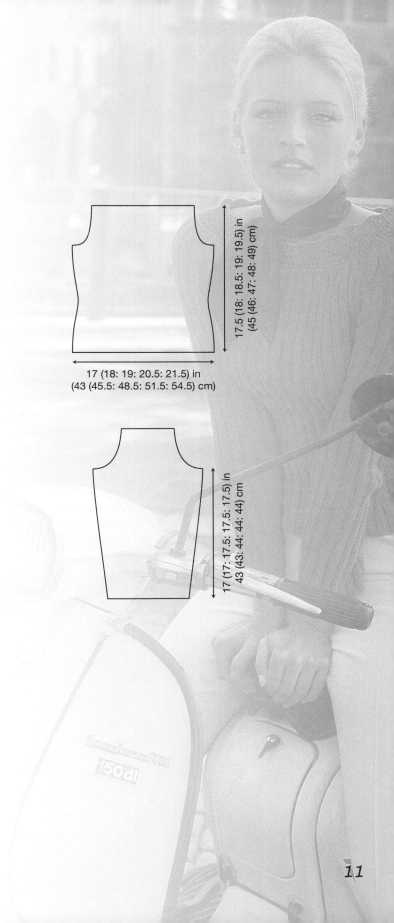

17.5 (18: 18.5: 19: 19.5) in
(45 (46: 47: 48: 49) cm)

17 (18: 19: 20.5: 21.5) in
(43 (45.5: 48.5: 51.5: 54.5) cm)

17 (17: 17.5: 17.5: 17.5) in
43 (43: 44: 44: 44) cm

Fern

Beautifully soft, Rowan *Kid Classic* also drapes very well. It knits up quicker than its ethereal cousin, *Kidsilk Haze*, and produces a delightfully cozy knitted fabric. The classic design here, knitted in reverse stockinette stitch, has a low crossover front, with a gentle frilled edging, creating a very feminine look.

YARN AND SIZES

	XS	S	M	L	XL	
To fit bust	32	34	36	38	40	in
	81	86	91	97	102	cm

Worsted (CYCA Medium) yarn
Rowan *Kid Classic* (70% lambswool, 25% kid mohair, 4% nylon; 153yd/50g)
in Lavender Ice 841

6	6	7	7	7	balls

NEEDLES
1 pair size 7 (4.5mm) needles
1 pair size 8 (5mm) needles

EXTRAS
1yd/1m of narrow ribbon and decorative pin fastener

GAUGE
19 sts and 25 rows to 4in/10cm measured over reverse stockinette stitch using size 8 (5mm) needles *or size necessary to obtain correct gauge.*

BACK

Cast on 77 (81: 87: 91: 97) sts using size 7 (4.5mm) needles.

Rows 1 to 4: Purl.

Change to size 8 (5mm) needles.

Beg with a P row, work in rev St st for 6 rows, ending with a WS row.

Next row (RS): P2, P2tog, P to last 4 sts, P2tog tbl, P2.

Working all side seam decreases as set by last row, cont in rev St st, dec 1 st at each end of every foll 6th row until 69 (73: 79: 83: 89) sts rem.

Work 13 rows, ending with a WS row.

Next row (RS): P2, M1, P to last 2 sts, M1, P2.

Working all side seam increases as set by last row, inc 1 st at each end of every foll 8th row to 75 (79: 85: 89: 95) sts, then on every foll 6th row until there are 83 (87: 93: 97: 103) sts.

Work 5 (7: 7: 9: 9) rows, ending with a WS row. (Back should measure 13 (14$\frac{1}{4}$: 14$\frac{1}{4}$: 14$\frac{1}{2}$: 14$\frac{1}{2}$) in/35 (36: 36: 37: 37)cm.)

Shape armholes

Bind off 3 (4: 4: 5: 5) sts at beg of next 2 rows. *77 (79: 85: 87: 93) sts.*

Dec 1 st at each end of next 5 (5: 7: 7: 9) rows, then on foll 3 alt rows. *61 (63: 65: 67: 69) sts.*

Cont even until armhole measures 7 (7: 7$\frac{1}{2}$: 7$\frac{1}{2}$: 8)in/18 (18: 19: 19: 20)cm, ending with a WS row.

Shape shoulders and back neck

Next row (RS): Bind off 4 (4: 4: 4: 5) sts, P until there are 11 (11: 12: 12: 12) sts on right needle and turn, leaving rem sts on a holder.

Work each side of neck separately.

Dec 1 st at beg of next row.

Bind off 4 (4: 4: 4: 5) sts at beg and dec 1 st at end of next row.

Dec 1 st at beg of next row.

Bind off rem 4 (4: 5: 5: 4) sts.

With RS facing, rejoin yarn to rem sts, bind off center 31 (33: 33: 35: 35) sts, P to end.

Complete to match first side, reversing shapings.

LEFT FRONT

Cast on 65 (67: 70: 72: 75) sts using size 7 (4.5mm) needles.

Row 1 (RS): P to last 13 sts, K13.

Row 2: K13, P to end.

Rows 3 and 4: As rows 1 and 2.

Change to size 8 (5mm) needles.

Row 5 (RS): P to last 13 sts, K13.

Row 6: Knit.

Last 2 rows set the sts—front opening edge 13 sts in garter st (for frill edging) and rem sts in rev St st.

Keeping sts correct as set, work 4 rows, ending with a WS row.

Working all side seam decreases as given for back, dec 1 st at beg of next and every foll 6th row until 61 (63: 66: 68: 71) sts rem.

Work 13 rows, ending with a WS row.

Working all side seam increases as given for back, inc 1 st at beg of next row.

62 (64: 67: 69: 72) sts.

Next row (WS): K1, [take yarn round needle and draw loop through st on right needle as though to K a st] 4 times (to create short chain), K12, wrap next st (by slipping next st to right needle, taking yarn to opposite side of work between needles and then slipping same st back onto left needle—when working back across sts work the wrapped loop tog with the wrapped st), turn, K13, turn, K1, [take yarn round needle and draw loop through st on right needle as though to K a st] 4 times (to create short chain), K to end.

Next row: P to last 13 sts, K13.

Next row: K1, [take yarn round needle and draw loop through st on right needle as though to K a st] 4 times (to create short chain), K to end.

Next row: P to last 13 sts, K13.

Last 4 rows set the sts—front opening edge 13

sts as frill edging and rem sts in rev St st.
Keeping sts correct as set, work 1 row, ending
with a WS row.

Shape front slope
Next row (RS): P to last 17 sts, P2tog tbl, P2, K13.
61 (63: 66: 68: 71) sts.
This row sets front slope decreases.
Working all front slope decreases as set by last
row, dec 1 st at front slope edge of 2nd and foll 18
(19: 19: 20: 20) alt rows **and at same time** inc 1 st
at side seam edge on 2nd and foll 8th row, then
on 4 foll 6th rows. *48 (49: 52: 53: 56) sts.*
Work 1 row, ending with a WS row. (Left front now
matches back to beg of armhole shaping.)

Shape armhole
Keeping sts correct, bind off 3 (4: 4: 5: 5) sts at
beg and dec 1 (1: 1: 1: 0) st at front slope edge of
next row. *44 (44: 47: 47: 51) sts.*
Work 1 row.
Dec 1 st at armhole edge of next 5 (5: 7: 7: 9)
rows, then on foll 3 alt rows **and at same time**
dec 1 st at front slope edge of next (next: 3rd: 3rd:
next) and every foll 4th row. *33 (33: 34: 34: 35) sts.*
Dec 1 st at front slope edge only on 2nd and every
foll 4th row until 26 (26: 27: 27: 28) sts rem.
Cont even until left front matches back to start of
shoulder shaping, ending with a WS row.

Shape shoulder
Bind off 4 (4: 4: 4: 5) sts at beg of next and foll alt
row, then 4 (4: 5: 5: 4) sts at beg of foll alt row.
14 sts.
Cont as set on these 14 sts until shorter edge
measures 4$\frac{1}{2}$ (4$\frac{3}{4}$: 4$\frac{3}{4}$: 5: 5)in/11 (12: 12: 13:
13)cm.
Bind off.

RIGHT FRONT
Cast on 65 (67: 70: 72: 75) sts using size 7
(4.5mm) needles.
Row 1 (RS): K13, P to end.

Row 2: P to last 13 sts, K13.

Row 3: K1, [take yarn round needle and draw loop through st on right needle as though to K a st] 4 times (to create short chain), K12, P to end.

Row 4: As row 2.

Change to size 8 (5mm) needles.

Row 5 (RS): K1, [take yarn round needle and draw loop through st on right needle as though to K a st] 4 times (to create short chain), K12, P to end.

Row 6: Knit.

Row 7: K1, [take yarn round needle and draw loop through st on right needle as though to K a st] 4 times (to create short chain), K12, wrap next st, turn, K13, turn, K1, [take yarn round needle and draw loop through st on right needle as though to K a st] 4 times (to create short chain), K12, P to end.

Row 8: Knit.

Last 4 rows set the sts—front opening edge 13 sts as frill edging and rem sts in rev St st.

Keeping sts correct as set, work 2 rows, ending with a WS row.

Working all sides seam decreases as given for back, dec 1 st at end of next and every foll 6th row until 61 (63: 66: 68: 71) sts rem.

Work 13 rows, ending with a WS row.

Working all side seam increases as given for back, inc 1 st at end of next row.

62 (64: 67: 69: 72) sts.

Work 5 rows, ending with a WS row.

Shape front slope

Next row (RS): Patt 13 sts, P2, P2tog, P to end.

61 (63: 66: 68: 71) sts.

This row sets front slope decreases.

Complete to match left front, reversing shapings.

SLEEVES (both alike)

Cast on 39 (39: 41: 43: 43) sts using size 7 (4.5mm) needles.

Rows 1 to 4: Purl.

Change to size 8 (5mm) needles.

Beg with a P row, work in rev St st for 16 rows, ending with a WS row.

Next row (RS): P2, M1, P to last 2 sts, M1, P2.

Working all increases as set by last row, inc 1 st at each end of every foll 8th (8th: 8th: 8th: 6th) row to 45 (55: 55: 57: 47) sts, then on every foll 10th (10th: 10th: 10th: 8th) row until there are 57 (59: 61: 63: 65) sts.

Cont even until sleeve measures 17 (17: 17^1/$_2$: 17^1/$_2$: 17^1/$_2$)in/43 (43: 44: 44: 44)cm, ending with a WS row.

Shape top

Bind off 3 (4: 4: 5: 5) sts at beg of next 2 rows.

51 (51: 53: 53: 55) sts.

Dec 1 st at each end of next 3 rows, then on foll

2 alt rows, then on every foll 4th row until 33 (33: 35: 35: 37) sts rem.

Work 1 row, ending with a WS row.

Dec 1 st at each end of next and every foll alt row to 29 sts, then on foll 3 rows, ending with a WS row.

Bind off rem 23 sts.

FINISHING

PRESS as described on the information page 138. Join both shoulder seams using back stitch, or mattress stitch if preferred. Join bound-off ends of frill strips, then sew shorter edge to back neck, easing in fullness.

See information page 138 for finishing instructions, setting in sleeves using the set-in method.

Cut ribbon into 2 equal lengths and attach one length to inside of left front opening edge, 14 sts on from actual edge and level with start of front slope shaping.

Attach other length to inside of right side seam, level with first length.

Tie ribbons together to hold left front in place, and fasten right front with a decorative pin.

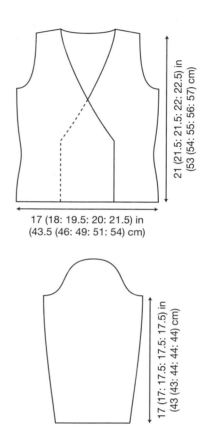

17 (18: 19.5: 20: 21.5) in (43.5 (46: 49: 51: 54) cm)

21 (21.5: 21.5: 22: 22.5) in (53 (54: 55: 56: 57) cm)

17 (17: 17.5: 17.5: 17.5) in (43 (43: 44: 44: 44) cm)

Brier

This classic jacket, with its set-in sleeves and rever collar, was originally knitted in Rowan *Yorkshire Tweed* but the new *Heritage Tweed* will substitute very well for this yarn. It has an attractive deep garter stitch border to the hem and the cuffs. The revers of the collar are whip-stitched in a contrasting shade for added effect and the sleeve seams are joined with wrong sides facing, so a neat ridge forms a detail on the right side. The corsage and gloves (see pages 24 and 26–27), in constrasting shades, make a pretty finishing touch to the ensemble.

YARN AND SIZES

	XS	S	M	L	XL	
To fit bust	32	34	36	38	40	in
	81	86	91	97	102	cm

DK (CYCA Light) yarn
Rowan *Heritage Tweed* (100% wool; 129yd/50g)
in Nappa 380

		9	9	9	10	10	balls

Remnants of *Heritage Tweed* in four shades and remnant of *Kidsilk Haze* for corsage. Remnant of *Fine Heritage Tweed* in Skipton 379 for embroidery. (Originally photographed in Rowan *Yorkshire Tweed DK* Sprinkle 353, embroidered with Rowan *Yorkshire Tweed 4ply* Sheer 267)

NEEDLES AND EXTRAS

1 pair size 3 (3.25mm) needles
1 pair size 5 (3.75mm) needles
1 pair size 6 (4mm) needles
Buttons: 3 x Rowan 00347 and 8 x Rowan 00316

GAUGE

20 sts and 28 rows to 4in/10cm measured over stockinette stitch using size 6 (4mm) needles *or size necessary to obtain correct gauge.*

YARN NOTE

This garment was knitted originally in Rowan *Yorkshire Tweed DK*. We suggest you substitute Rowan *Heritage Tweed*, which knits to a very similar gauge. However, make sure you do a gauge swatch and, if necessary, adapt your needle size (up or down) to achieve the gauge on the pattern. For further information, see page 140.

Pattern note: As row end edges form actual finished center back, front opening, back sleeve, and collar edges of garment, it is important these edges are kept neat. Therefore avoid joining in new balls of yarn at these edges.

BACK
Right back
Cast on 47 (49: 52: 54: 57) sts using size 3 (3.25mm) needles.

Work in garter st for 3in/8cm, ending with a WS row.

(Ends of RS rows form center back and, as center back seam is sewn with WS together so that seam forms a ridge, this is edge to keep neat.)

Change to size 6 (4mm) needles.

Beg with a K row, cont in St st as foll:

Work 10 rows, ending with a WS row.

Counting in from center back edge, place marker on 24th (25th: 26th: 27th: 28th) st in from center back.

Next row (dec) (RS): K2, K2tog, K to within 1 st of marked st, right dec, K to end.

44 (46: 49: 51: 54) sts.

Work 7 rows.

Rep last 8 rows once more, then first of these rows (the dec row) again. *38 (40: 43: 45: 48) sts.*

Cont even until right back measures 9¼ (9½: 9½: 10: 10)in/23.5 (24.5: 24.5: 25.5: 25.5)cm ending with a WS row.

Next row (inc) (RS): K2, M1, K to marked st, M1, K marked st, M1, K to end. *41 (43: 46: 48: 51) sts.*

Work 11 rows.

Rep last 12 rows once more, then first of these rows (the inc row) again. *47 (49: 52: 54: 57) sts.*

Work 21 rows, ending with a WS row. (Right back

should measure 15¾ (16: 16: 16½: 16½)in/40 (41: 41: 42: 42)cm.)

Shape armhole
Bind off 3 (4: 4: 5: 5) sts at beg of next row.

44 (45: 48: 49: 52) sts.

Work 1 row.

Dec 1 st at armhole edge of next 5 (5: 7: 7: 9) rows, then on foll 4 alt rows. *35 (36: 37: 38: 39) sts.*

Cont even until armhole measures 8 (8: 8¼: 8¼: 8¾)in/20 (20: 21: 21: 22)cm ending with a WS row.

Shape shoulder and back neck
Bind off 7 sts at beg of next row, then 11 (12: 12: 13: 13) sts at beg of foll row.

Bind off 7 sts at beg of next row, then 4 sts at beg of foll row.

Bind off rem 6 (6: 7: 7: 8) sts.

Left back
Cast on 47 (49: 52: 54: 57) sts using size 3 (3.25mm) needles.

Work in garter st for 3in/8cm, ending with a WS row.

(Ends of WS rows form center back and, as center back seam is sewn with WS together so that seam forms a ridge, this is edge to keep neat.)

Change to size 6 (4mm) needles.

Beg with a K row, cont in St st as foll:

Work 10 rows, ending with a WS row.

Counting in from center back edge, place marker on 24th (25th: 26th: 27th: 28th) st in from center back.

Next row (dec) (RS): K to within 1 st of marked st, left dec, K to last 4 sts, K2tog tbl, K2.

44 (46: 49: 51: 54) sts.

Complete to match right back, reversing shapings.

LEFT FRONT
Cast on 51 (53: 56: 58: 61) sts using size 3 (3.25mm) needles.

SPECIAL ABBREVIATIONS
Right dec = skp, slip st now on right needle back onto left needle, lift second st on left needle over first st and off left needle, then slip same st back onto right needle—2 sts decreased.

Left dec = sk2p (marked st is first of these 2 sts)—2 sts decreased.

Work in garter st for 3in/8cm, ending with a WS row.

(Ends of RS rows form front opening edge and this is edge to keep neat.)

Change to size 6 (4mm) needles.

Working a sl st edging as described on the information page 138 at front opening edge (end of RS rows and beg of WS rows), cont in St st, beg with a K row, as foll:

Work 10 rows, ending with a WS row.

Counting in from front opening edge, place marker on 28th (29th: 30th: 31st: 32nd) st in from front opening edge.

Next row (dec) (RS): K2, K2tog, K to within 1 st of marked st, right dec, patt to end.
48 (50: 53: 55: 58) sts.

Work 7 rows.

Rep last 8 rows once more, then first of these rows (the dec row) again. *42 (44: 47: 49: 52) sts.*

Cont even until left front measures 9¼ (9½: 9½: 10: 10)in/23.5 (24.5: 24.5: 25.5: 25.5)cm, ending with a WS row.

Next row (inc) (RS): K2, M1, K to marked st, M1, K marked st, M1, K to end. *45 (47: 50: 52: 55) sts.*

Work 11 rows.

Rep last 12 rows once more, then first of these rows (the inc row) again. *51 (53: 56: 58: 61) sts.*

Work 1 row, ending with a WS row.

Shape for lapel

Next row (RS): K to last 2 sts, M1, patt to end.

Working all lapel increases as set by last row, inc 1 st at end of foll 10th row. *53 (55: 58: 60: 63) sts.*

Work 9 rows, ending with a WS row. (Left front now matches back to beg of armhole shaping.)

Shape armhole

Bind off 3 (4: 4: 5: 5) sts at beg and inc 1 st at end of next row. *51 (52: 55: 56: 59) sts.*

Work 1 row.

Dec 1 st at armhole edge of next 5 (5: 7: 7: 9) rows, then on foll 4 alt rows **and at same time** inc

1 st at lapel edge of 9th row. *43 (44: 45: 46: 47) sts.*

Inc 1 st at lapel edge of 6th (6th: 4th: 4th: 2nd) and foll 10th row. *45 (46: 47: 48: 49) sts.*

Cont even until 15 (15: 15: 17: 17) rows fewer have been worked than on right back to start of shoulder shaping, ending with a RS row.

Next row (WS): Patt 1 st, K16 (17: 17: 17: 17), P to end.

Work 1 row.

Next row: Patt 1 st, K17 (18: 18: 18: 18), P to end.

Shape neck

Next row (RS): K27 (27: 28: 29: 30), bind off rem 18 (19: 19: 19: 19) sts.

Rejoin yarn with WS facing.

Dec 1 st at neck edge of next 4 rows, then on foll 3 (3: 3: 4: 4) alt rows. *20 (20: 21: 21: 22) sts.*

Work 1 row, ending with a WS row.

Shape shoulder

Bind off 7 sts at beg of next and foll alt row.

Work 1 row. Bind off rem 6 (6: 7: 7: 8) sts.

Mark positions for 3 buttons along left front opening edge—first button to come level with row 15 of St st section above garter st border, last button to come 2½in/6cm down from start of lapel shaping and rem button midway between.

RIGHT FRONT

Cast on 51 (53: 56: 58: 61) sts using size 3 (3.25mm) needles.

Work in garter st for 3in/8cm, ending with a WS row.

(Ends of WS rows form front opening edge and this is edge to keep neat.)

Change to size 6 (4mm) needles.

Working a sl st edging as described on the information page 138 at front opening edge (end of WS rows and beg of RS rows), cont in St st, beg with a K row, as foll:

Work 10 rows, ending with a WS row.

Counting in from front opening edge, place

marker on 28th (29th: 30th: 31st: 32nd) st in from front opening edge.

Next row (dec) (RS): Patt to within 1 st of marked st, left dec, K to last 4 sts, K2tog tbl, K2.
48 (50: 53: 55: 58) sts.

Work 3 rows, ending with a WS row.

Next row (buttonhole row) (RS): Patt 3 sts, bind off 3 sts (to make a buttonhole—cast on 3 sts over these bound-off sts on next row), K to end.

Complete to match left front, reversing shapings and with the addition of a further 2 buttonholes worked in same way as first to correspond with positions marked on left front for buttons.

LEFT SLEEVE
Back sleeve
Cast on 18 (18: 19: 20: 20) sts using size 3 (3.25mm) needles.

Work in garter st for 2$\frac{1}{2}$in/6cm, ending with a WS row.

(Ends of RS rows form back sleeve seam and, as this seam is sewn with WS together so that seam forms a ridge, this is edge to keep neat.)

Next row (RS): K2, M1, K to end.
19 (19: 20: 21: 21) sts.

Cont in garter st until sleeve measures 4$\frac{1}{2}$in/11cm, ending with a RS row.

Bind off 4 sts at beg of next row.
15 (15: 16: 17: 17) sts.

Change to size 6 (4mm) needles.

Beg with a K row, cont in St st as foll:

Work 2 rows, ending with a WS row.

Next row (RS): K2, M1, K to end.

Working all increases as set by last row, inc 1 st at beg (underarm seam edge) of every foll 14th (12th: 12th: 12th: 10th) row to 19 (21: 21: 22: 22) sts, then on every foll 16th (14th: 14th: 14th: 12th) row until there are 21 (22: 23: 24: 25) sts.

Cont even until back sleeve measures 17 (17: 17$\frac{1}{2}$: 17$\frac{1}{2}$: 17$\frac{1}{2}$)in/43 (43: 44: 44: 44)cm, ending with a WS row.

Shape top
Bind off 3 (4: 4: 5: 5) sts at beg of next row.
18 (18: 19: 19: 20) sts.

Work 1 row.

Dec 1 st at beg of next row and at same edge on foll 2 rows, then on foll 3 alt rows, then on every foll 4th row until 8 (8: 9: 9: 10) sts rem.

Work 1 row, ending with a WS row.

Dec 1 st at beg of next and every foll alt row until 4 sts rem, then dec 1 st at shaped edge on foll 3 rows.

Fasten off rem 1 st.

Front sleeve

Cast on 39 (39: 40: 41: 41) sts using size 3 (3.25mm) needles.

Work in garter st for 2½in/6cm, ending with a WS row.

(Ends of WS rows form back sleeve seam and, as this seam is sewn with WS together so that seam forms a ridge, this is edge to keep neat.)

Next row (RS): K to last 2 sts, M1, K2.

40 (40: 41: 42: 42) sts.

Cont in garter st until sleeve measures 4½in/11cm, ending with a WS row.

Change to size 6 (4mm) needles.

Beg with a K row, cont in St st as foll:

Work 2 rows, ending with a WS row.

Next row (RS): K to last 2 sts, M1, K2.

Working all increases as set by last row, inc 1 st at end (underarm seam edge) of every foll 14th (12th: 12th: 12th: 10th) row to 44 (46: 46: 47: 47) sts, then on every foll 16th (14th: 14th: 14th: 12th) row until there are 46 (47: 48: 49: 50) sts.

Cont even until front sleeve measures 17 (17: 17½: 17½: 17½)in/43 (43: 44: 44: 44)cm, ending with a RS row.

Shape top

Bind off 3 (4: 4: 5: 5) sts at beg of next row.

43 (43: 44: 44: 45) sts.

Dec 1 st at end of next row and at same edge on foll 2 rows, then on foll 3 alt rows, then on every foll 4th row until 33 (33: 34: 34: 35) sts rem.

Work 1 row, ending with a WS row.

Dec 1 st at end of next and every foll alt row until 29 sts rem, then dec 1 st at shaped edge on foll 2 rows, ending with a RS row. *27 sts.*

Dec 1 st at each end of next 3 rows.

Bind off rem 21 sts.

RIGHT SLEEVE
Front sleeve

Cast on 39 (39: 40: 41: 41) sts using size 3 (3.25mm) needles.

Work in garter st for 2½in/6cm, ending with a WS row.

(Ends of RS rows form back sleeve seam and, as this seam is sewn with WS together so that seam forms a ridge, this is edge to keep neat.)

Next row (RS): K2, M1, K to end.

40 (40: 41: 42: 42) sts.

Complete to match left front sleeve, reversing shapings.

Back sleeve

Cast on 18 (18: 19: 20: 20) sts using size 3 (3.25mm) needles.

Work in garter st for 2½in/6cm, ending with a WS row.

(Ends of WS rows form back sleeve seam and, as this seam is sewn with WS together so that seam forms a ridge, this is edge to keep neat.)

Next row (RS): K to last 2 sts, M1, K2.

19 (19: 20: 21: 21) sts.

Cont in garter st until sleeve measures 4½in/11cm, ending with a WS row.

Change to size 6 (4mm) needles.

Beg with a K row, cont in St st as foll:

Bind off 4 sts at beg of next row.

15 (15: 16: 17: 17) sts.

Work 1 row, ending with a WS row.

Next row (RS): K2, M1, K to end.

Complete to match left back sleeve, reversing shapings.

FINISHING

PRESS as described on the information page 138.

Join both shoulder seams using back stitch, or mattress stitch if preferred.

Collar

Cast on 72 (78: 78: 86: 86) sts using size 5 (3.75mm) needles.

Work in garter st for 4 rows, ending with a WS row.

Change to size 6 (4mm) needles.

Next row (RS): K3, P to last 3 sts, K3.
Next row: Knit.
Rep last 2 rows 3 times more.
Next row (RS): P2, P2tog tbl, P to last 4 sts, P2tog, P2.
Next row: Knit.
Rep last 2 rows 4 times more.
62 (68: 68: 76: 76) sts.
Bind off 6 (7: 7: 8: 8) sts at beg of next 2 rows, then 7 (8: 8: 9: 9) sts at beg of foll 4 rows.
Bind off rem 22 (22: 22: 24: 24) sts.
Stitching seam with WS together so that ridge is formed on RS, join backs and sleeves as foll:
Sew center back seam, leaving first 3in/8cm open for back vent. Sew sleeve sections together, leaving first 4½in/11cm open for cuff vent. Sew bound-off edge in place under front sleeve, then attach 4 buttons to each cuff through both layers, using photograph as a guide.
Stitching seam with RS of body against WS of collar (so that ridge is formed on inside of body and therefore visible when lapel is turned back), sew shaped bound-off edge of collar to neck edge and shaped row-end edges of collar to lapel bound-off sts, leaving approx 1½in/4cm free.
See information page 138 for finishing instructions, setting in sleeves using the set-in method.
Using contrast yarn and photograph as a guide, oversew along front opening and collar edges.

Corsage
BACK SECTION
Using size 6 (4mm) needles and first shade of *Heritage Tweed*, cast on 22 sts.
Beg with a K row and working in 2 row stripes of first and second shades, cont in St st until work is a perfect square.
Bind off.

FRONT SECTION

Work as for back section but using third and fourth shades of *Heritage Tweed*.

CENTER SECTION

Cast on 6 sts using *Kidsilk Haze* DOUBLE and size 6 (4mm) needles.
Cont in rev St st, inc 1 st at end of next 6 rows.
12 sts.
Dec 1 st at end of next 6 rows. *6 sts.*
Bind off.

FINISHING

Machine hot wash and tumble dry back and front sections to shrink and felt them. Once dry, press. From back section, cut a 3in/8cm diameter circle, and from front section, cut a 2½in/6cm diameter circle. Run gathering threads around outer edge of center section and pull up so that center section forms a soft, flat ball. Fasten ends off securely. Lay front section onto back section, and run gathering threads through both layers around center point. Pull up threads so that sections form a rumpled flower shape and fasten ends off securely. Position center section over these gathering threads and sew all 3 sections together at center. If desired, attach a safety pin or brooch back to back of corsage.

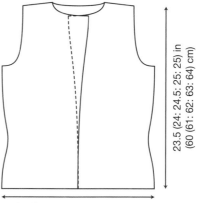

23.5 (24: 24.5: 25: 25) in
(60 (61: 62: 63: 64) cm)

18.5 (19.5: 20.5: 21.5: 22.5) in
(47 (49: 52: 54: 57) cm)

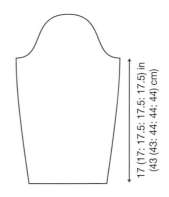

17 (17: 17.5: 17.5: 17.5) in
(43 (43: 44: 44: 44) cm)

Fawne

YARN AND SIZES
One size, to fit average size adult hand
4ply (CYCA Superfine) yarn
Rowan *Cashsoft 4ply* (57% fine merino wool,
33% microfiber, 10% cashmere; 197yd/50g)
A   Cherish 453   1 ball
B   Elite 451   1 ball
(Originally photographed in Rowan *4ply Soft*
Raincloud 387 and Sooty 372)

NEEDLES
1 pair size 2 (2.75mm) needles

GAUGE
32 sts and 40 rows to 4in/10cm measured over
stockinette stitch using size 2 (2.75mm) needles
or size necessary to obtain correct gauge.

YARN NOTE
This garment was originally knitted in Rowan
4ply Soft. We suggest you substitute Rowan
Cashsoft 4ply, which knits to a very similar gauge.
However, make sure you do a gauge swatch and,
if necessary, adapt your needle size (up or down)
to achieve the gauge on the pattern. If you do
not, even a couple of stitches/rows difference on
a thick yarn over a 4in/10cm swatch will make a
noticeable difference to the width/length of the
garment. For further information, see page 140.

RIGHT GLOVE
Cast on 54 sts using size 2 (2.75mm) needles and
yarn A.
Row 1 (RS): K2, *P2, K2, rep from * to end.
Row 2: P2, *K2, P2, rep from * to end.
These 2 rows form rib.
Join in yarn B.
Using yarn B, work 2 rows.
Using yarn A, work 2 rows.
Last 4 rows form stripe sequence.

Keeping stripes correct throughout, cont as foll:
Cont in rib until work measures 3in/8cm, ending with a WS row.
Beg with a K row, work in St st for 6 rows.**

Shape thumb
Row 1 (RS): K28, inc in next st, K2, inc in next st, K22. *56 sts.*
Work 3 rows.
Row 5: K28, inc in next st, K4, inc in next st, K22. *58 sts.*
Work 3 rows.
Row 9: K28, inc in next st, K6, inc in next st, K22. *60 sts.*
Work 3 rows.
Cont in this way, inc 2 sts on next and every foll 4th row until there are 68 sts.
Work 3 rows, ending with a WS row.
Next row (RS): K46, turn and cast on 2 sts.
Next row: P20, turn and cast on 2 sts.
***Work 1¼in/3cm on these 22 sts only for thumb.
Bind off. Sew thumb seam.
With RS facing, rejoin appropriate yarn and pick up and knit 6 sts from base of thumb, K to end. *56 sts.*
Cont even until work measures 1½in/4cm from pick-up row, ending with a WS row.

Shape first finger
Next row (RS): K36, turn and cast on 1 st.
Next row: P17, turn and cast on 1 st.
Work 1¼in/3cm on these 18 sts only for first finger.
Bind off. Sew seam.

Shape second finger
With RS facing, rejoin appropriate yarn and pick up and knit 2 sts from base of first finger, K7, turn and cast on 1 st.
Next row: P17, turn and cast on 1 st.
Work 1¼in/3cm on these 18 sts only for second finger.
Bind off. Sew seam.

Shape third finger
With RS facing, rejoin appropriate yarn and pick up and knit 2 sts from base of second finger, K7, turn and cast on 1 st.
Next row: P17, turn and cast on 1 st.
Work 1¼in/3cm on these 18 sts only for third finger.
Bind off. Sew seam.

Shape fourth finger
With RS facing, rejoin appropriate yarn and pick up and knit 4 sts from base of third finger, K to end.
Next row: P16.
Work 1¼in/3cm on these 16 sts only for fourth finger.
Bind off. Sew finger and side seam.

LEFT GLOVE
Work as given for right glove to **.

Shape thumb
Row 1 (RS): K22, inc in next st, K2, inc in next st, K28. *56 sts.*
Work 3 rows.
Row 5: K22, inc in next st, K4, inc in next st, K28. *58 sts.*
Work 3 rows.
Row 9: K22, inc in next st, K6, inc in next st, K28. *60 sts.*
Work 3 rows.
Cont in this way, inc 2 sts on next and every foll 4th row until there are 68 sts.
Work 3 rows, ending with a WS row.
Next row (RS): K40, turn and cast on 2 sts.
Next row: P20, turn and cast on 2 sts.
Complete as given for right glove from ***.

FINISHING
PRESS as described on the information page 138.

Ash

This softly ribbed and lacy design makes a wonderfully simple but luxurious cover-up for a cooler day in summer. The wrap is drawn in at the waist with a knitted tie, threaded through the eyelet holes. Using the light and ethereal *Kidsilk Haze* yarn double makes quicker work of the knitting and adds body to the garment. The pattern is really not difficult to knit, making a great introduction to textured stitches.

YARN AND SIZES

	XS	S–M	L–XL	
To fit bust	32	34–36	38–40	in
	81	86–91	97–102	cm

Lightweight (CYCA Fine) yarn
*Rowan *Kidsilk Haze* (70% super kid mohair, 30% silk; 229yd/25g) in Meadow 581

	5	6	6	balls

*Use DOUBLE throughout

NEEDLES
1 pair size 3 (3.25mm) needles
1 pair size 5 (3.75mm) needles
2 double-pointed size 3 (3.25mm) needles

GAUGE
22 sts and 32 rows to 4in/10cm measured over pattern using size 5 (3.75mm) needles and yarn DOUBLE *or size necessary to obtain correct gauge*.

TOP

Right front

Cast on 56 (60: 64) sts using size 5 (3.75mm) needles and yarn DOUBLE.

Row 1 (RS): K2, *P1, K1, rep from * to end.
Row 2: *P1, K1, rep from * to end.
These 2 rows form rib.
Cont in rib for 5in/12cm, ending with a WS row.
Next row (eyelet row) (RS): K2, *yo, K2tog, P1, K1, rep from * to last 2 sts, P1, K1.
Work in rib for a further 2 rows, ending with a RS row.
Next row (WS): K4 (2: 4), M1, *K6 (7: 7), M1, rep from * to last 4 (2: 4) sts, K to end. *65 (69: 73) sts.*
Cont in patt as foll:
Row 1 (RS): P1, *P2, yo, P2tog, rep from * to end.
Row 2: *K2, yo, skp, rep from * to last st, K1.
These 2 rows form patt.
Cont in patt until right front measures 19³/₄ (20: 20¹/₂)in/50 (51: 52)cm, ending with a WS row.

Shape back

Place marker at beg of last row.
Cont in patt until work measures 4in/10cm from marker, ending with a WS row.
Break yarn and leave sts on a holder.

Left front

Cast on 56 (60: 64) sts using size 5 (3.75mm) needles and yarn DOUBLE.

Row 1 (RS): *K1, P1, rep from * to last 2 sts, K2.
Row 2: *K1, P1, rep from * to end.
These 2 rows form rib.
Cont in rib for 5in/12cm, ending with a WS row.
Next row (eyelet row) (RS): [K1, P1] twice, K1, *yo, K2tog, P1, K1, rep from * to last 3 sts, yo, K2tog, K1.
Work in rib for a further 2 rows, ending with a RS row.
Next row (WS): K4 (2: 4), M1, *K6 (7: 7), M1, rep from * to last 4 (2: 4) sts, K to end. *65 (69: 73) sts.*
Cont in patt as foll:

Row 1 (RS): *P2, yo, P2tog, rep from * to last st, P1.
Row 2: K1, *K2, yo, skp, rep from * to end.
These 2 rows form patt.
Cont in patt until left front measures 19³/₄ (20: 20¹/₂)in/50 (51: 52)cm, ending with a WS row.

Shape back

Place marker at end of last row.
Cont in patt until work measures 4in/10cm from marker, ending with a WS row.

Join sections

Next row (RS): Patt across first 63 (67: 71) sts of left front, P2tog, then patt across 65 (69: 73) sts of right front as foll: P2tog, patt to end.
128 (136: 144) sts.
Cont in patt across all sts until back measures 14¹/₂ (15: 15¹/₄)in/37 (38: 39)cm from markers, ending with a RS row.
Next row (WS): K0 (4: 8), K2tog, *K7, K2tog, rep from * to last 0 (4: 8) sts, K0 (4: 8).
113 (121: 129) sts.
Next row: P1, *K1, P1, rep from * to end.
Next row: K1, *P1, K1, rep from * to end.
These 2 rows form rib.
Next row (eyelet row) (RS): P1, K1, *yo, K2tog, P1, K1, rep from * to last 3 sts, yo, K2tog, P1.
Cont in rib until back measures 19³/₄ (20: 20¹/₂)in/50 (51: 52)cm from markers, ending with a WS row.
Bind off in rib.

FINISHING

PRESS as described on the information page 138.

Armhole borders (both alike)
Mark points along side edges 8³/₄ (9: 9¹/₂)in/22 (23: 24)cm either side of shoulder markers.
With RS facing, using size 3 (3.25mm) needles and yarn DOUBLE, pick up and knit 94 (98: 102) sts evenly along edge between these markers.
Bind off knitwise (on WS).
Join side seams below armhole borders.

Tie

With double-pointed size 3 (3.25mm) needles and yarn SINGLE, cast on 4 sts.

Row 1 (RS): K4, *without turning work slip these 4 sts to opposite end of needle and bring yarn to opposite end of work pulling it quite tightly across back of these 4 sts, using other needle K these 4 sts again; rep from * until tie is 47$\frac{1}{4}$ (51$\frac{1}{4}$:55) in/120 (130: 140)cm long.

Bind off.

Thread tie through eyelet holes at top of rib.

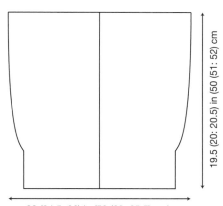

19.5 (20: 20.5) in (50 (51: 52) cm)

23 (24.5: 26) in (58 (62: 65.5) cm)

Garth

This is the classic, rugged, polo neck sweater. It has a man's and a woman's version. Easy and very fast to knit in stockinette stitch in a chunky yarn, such as Rowan's *British Sheep Breeds DK* used double, it was originally designed in Rowan *Plaid*, a similarly flecked thick yarn, reminiscent of the undyed, oiled wool yarns used in traditional fisherman's sweaters. The replacement *British Sheep Breeds* yarn comes even closer to matching these traditional yarns. If you don't want the natural fleck, then opt for Bluefaced Leicester (a plain cream) or the Brown Bluefaced Leicester (a natural soft brown).

YARN AND SIZES

	ladies			mens			
	S	M	L	M	L	XL	
To fit bust/chest	34	36	38	40	42	44	in
	86	91	97	102	107	112	cm

DK (CYCA Light) yarn
*Rowan *British Sheep Breeds DK* (100% wool; 131yd/50g)

	12	13	14	12	13	14	balls

* Use DOUBLE throughout
Ladies': Bluefaced Leicester Grey Suffolk 784
Men's: Bluefaced Leicester Marl 783
(Originally photographed in Rowan *Plaid* in ladies': Creeper 155; men's: Seagull 167)

NEEDLES AND EXTRAS

1 pair size 10¹/₂ (7mm) needles
1 pair size 11 (8mm) needles
Buttons: 3 x Rowan 00359 for ladies' version only

GAUGE

11 sts and 15 rows to 4in/10cm measured over stockinette stitch using size 11 (8mm) needles *or size necessary to obtain correct gauge.*

YARN NOTE

This garment was knitted originally in Rowan *Plaid*. We suggest you substitute Rowan *British Sheep Breeds DK*, which knits to a very similar gauge. However, make sure you do a gauge swatch and, if necessary, adapt your needle size (up or down) to achieve the gauge on the pattern. If you do not, even a couple of stitches/rows difference on a thick yarn over a 4in/10cm swatch will make a noticeable difference to the width/length of the garment. For further information, see page 140.

Pattern note: The pattern is written for the 3 ladies' sizes, followed by the men's sizes in **bold**. Where only one figure appears this applies to all sizes in that group.

Beg with a K row, cont in St st until back measures 17³/₄ (**15¹/₂**)in/45 (**39**)cm, ending with a WS row.

Shape raglan armholes
Bind off 5 (**6**) sts at beg of next 2 rows.
*51 (53: 55: **53: 55: 57**) sts.*
Next row (RS): P1, K1, P1, K2tog, K to last 5 sts, K2tog tbl, P1, K1, P1.
Next row: K1, P1, K1, P to last 3 sts, K1, P1, K1.
Rep last 2 rows 14 (15: 16: **16: 17: 18**) times more.
*21 (**19**) sts.*
Next row (RS): P1, K1, P1, K2tog, K to last 5 sts, K2tog tbl, P1, K1, P1.
Next row: K1, P1, K1, P2tog tbl, P to last 5 sts, P2tog, K1, P1, K1.
Bind off rem 17 (**15**) sts.

FRONT
Work as given for back until 25 (**23**) sts rem in raglan armhole shaping.
Work 1 row, ending with a WS row.
Shape neck
Next row (RS): P1, K1, P1, K2tog, K1 and turn, leaving rem sts on a holder.
Work each side of neck separately.
Next row: P2tog, K1, P1, K1.
Next row: P1, K1, P2tog.
Next row: P2tog tbl, K1.
Next row: P2tog and fasten off.
With RS facing, rejoin yarn to rem sts, bind off center 13 (**11**) sts (one st on right needle), K2tog tbl, P1, K1, P1. *5 sts.*
Complete to match first side, reversing shapings.

SLEEVES
Cast on 37 sts using size 10¹/₂ (7mm) needles.
Row 1 (RS): P2, *K3, P2, rep from * to end.
Row 2: K2, *P3, K2, rep from * to end.
Rep last 2 rows 7 times more, ending with a WS row.

BACK
Cast on 61 (63: 65: **65: 67: 69**) sts using size 10¹/₂ (7mm) needles.
Row 1 (RS): K2 (0: 0: **0: 0: 1**), P2 (0: 1: **1: 2: 2**), *K3, P2, rep from * to last 2 (3: 4: **4: 0: 1**) sts, K2 (3: 3: **3: 0: 1**), P0 (0: 1: **1: 0: 0**).
Row 2: P2 (0: 0: **0: 0: 1**), K2 (0: 1: **1: 2: 2**), *P3, K2, rep from * to last 2 (3: 4: **4: 0: 1**) sts, P2 (3: 3: **3: 0: 1**), K0 (0: 1: **1: 0: 0**).
Rep last 2 rows 8 (**6**) times more, ending with a WS row.
Change to size 11 (8mm) needles.

Change to size 11 (8mm) needles.

Beg with a K row, cont in St st as foll:

Work 2 rows, ending with a WS row.

Next row (inc) (RS): K2, M1, K to last 2 sts, M1, K2.

Working all increases as set by last row, inc 1 st at each end of every foll 10th (8th: 6th: **6th: 6th: 4th**) row to 47 (45: 41: **45: 51: 41**) sts, then on every foll - (10th: 8th: **8th: 8th: 6th**) row until there are - (49: 51: **53: 55: 57**) sts.

Cont even until sleeve measures 17¼ (18: 19: **19¾: 20: 20½**)in/44 (46: 48: **50: 51: 52**)cm, ending with a WS row.

Shape raglan

Bind off 5 (**6**) sts at beg of next 2 rows.

*37 (39: 41: **41: 43: 45**) sts.*

Next row (RS): P1, K1, P1, K2tog, K to last 5 sts, K2tog tbl, P1, K1, P1.

Next row: K1, P1, K1, P to last 3 sts, K1, P1, K1.

Next row: P1, K1, P1, K to last 3 sts, P1, K1, P1.

Next row: K1, P1, K1, P to last 3 sts, K1, P1, K1.

Rep last 4 rows 1 (**0**) times more.

*33 (35: 37: **39: 41: 43**) sts.*

Next row (RS): P1, K1, P1, K2tog, K to last 5 sts, K2tog tbl, P1, K1, P1.

Next row: K1, P1, K1, P to last 3 sts, K1, P1, K1.

Rep last 2 rows 10 (11: 12: **14: 15: 16**) times more.

*11 (**9**) sts.*

Left sleeve only

Next row (RS): P1, K1, P1, K2tog, K to last 5 sts, K2tog tbl, P1, K1, P1. *9 (**7**) sts.*

Bind off 4 (**3**) sts at beg of next row.

Right sleeve only

Next row (RS): Bind off 5 sts (one st on right needle), [K2tog tbl] 1 (**0**) times, P1, K1, P1.

Work 1 row.

Both sleeves

Bind off rem 5 (**4**) sts.

FINISHING

PRESS as described on the information page 138.

Special tips

ALTERNATIVE NECKLINE

On a classic design such as this sweater, there is no reason why you cannot change the neckline if you wish. To make it into a crew neck sweater, simply follow the instructions given for the polo neck collar—but bind off after you have worked just 5 or 6 rows in the rib pattern. Or try a more casual neckline, by working an inch or so in stockinette stitch. Pick up the number of sts given for the polo neck using size 11 (8mm) needles and simply work in stockinette stitch, beg with a P row, until the new neckline is the required length. This type of neckline will create a little "roll" at the upper edge, giving a much more relaxed feel to the sweater. Whatever type of neckline you choose to knit, make sure you bind off loosely so that you can easily get your head through the opening! It is often a good idea to bind off using a needle one or two sizes larger than used for the neckband as this forms a more elastic edge.

Ladies' sweater only

Join raglan seams using back stitch, or mattress stitch if preferred.

Collar

Cast on 88 sts using size 11 (8mm) needles.

Row 1 (RS): K1, [K1, P1] 3 times, *K3, P2, rep from * to last 6 sts, [K1, P1] twice, K2.

Row 2: (K1, P1) 3 times, *K2, P3, rep from * to last 7 sts, [K1, P1] 3 times, K1.

These 2 rows form rib.

Cont in rib until collar measures 2in/5cm, ending with a WS row.

Next row (buttonhole row) (RS): K2, P1, yo, P2tog, rib to end.

Cont in rib until collar measures 4in/10cm, ending with a WS row.

Rep the buttonhole row once more.

Change to size 10½ (7mm) needles.

Cont in rib until collar measures 6in/15cm, ending with a WS row.

Rep the buttonhole row once more.

Work 3 rows, ending with a WS row.

Next row (RS): K1, [K1, P1] 3 times, *K1, K2tog tbl, P2, rep from * to last 6 sts, [K1, P1] twice, K2. *73 sts.*

Next row: [K1, P1] 3 times, *K2, P2, rep from * to last 7 sts, [K1, P1] 3 times, K1.

Next row: P1, (K1, P1) 3 times, *K2, P2, rep from * to last 6 sts, [K1, P1] 3 times.

Rep last 2 rows until collar measures 10¼in/26cm.

Bind off in rib.

Overlap ends of collar for 6 sts and sew together at bound-off edge, ensuring end with buttonholes is against RS of other end. Positioning overlapped edge level with left front raglan seam, sew bound-off edge of collar to neck edge. Sew on buttons.

Men's sweater only

Join both front and right back raglan seams using back stitch, or mattress stitch if preferred.

Collar

With RS facing and using size 10¹/₂ (7mm) needles, pick up and knit 8 sts from top of left sleeve, 21 sts from front, 8 sts from right sleeve, then 15 sts from back. *52 sts.*

Beg with row 1, work in rib as given for sleeves for 3in/8cm.

Change to size 11 (8mm) needles.

Cont in rib until collar measures 8in/20cm.
Bind off in rib.
Join left back raglan and collar seam, reversing collar seam for turn-back.

All sweaters

See information page 138 for finishing instructions.

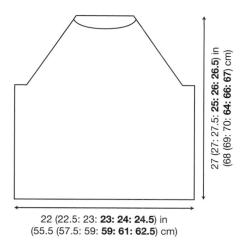

22 (22.5: 23: **23: 24: 24.5**) in
(55.5 (57.5: 59: **59: 61: 62.5**) cm)

27 (27: 27.5: **25: 26: 26.5**) in
(68 (69: 70: **64: 66: 67**) cm)

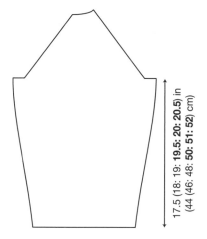

17.5 (18: 19: **19.5: 20: 20.5**) in
(44 (46: 48: **50: 51: 52**) cm)

Prue

This great classic sweater has perennial appeal, turning effortlessly from elegant to sporty, depending on how it is worn. Knitted in a 4-ply yarn in a great lacy pattern, the welt, cuffs, and neat collar are edged in a contrasting color to provide a smart finishing touch and the split neck fastens with delicate pearl buttons.

YARN AND SIZES

	XS	S	M	L	XL	
To fit bust	32	34	36	38	40	in
	81	86	91	97	102	cm

4ply (CYCA Super Fine) yarn
Rowan *Siena* (100% mercerized cotton; 153yd/50g)

A Celadan 669	10	11	11	12	12	balls
B Cream 652	1	1	1	1	1	ball

(Originally photographed in Rowan *4ply Cotton* in Fennel 135 and Fresh 131)

NEEDLES

1 pair size 1 (2.25mm) needles
1 pair size 3 (3mm) needles

EXTRAS

Buttons: 5 x Rowan 75320

GAUGE

28 sts and 40 rows to 4in/10cm measured over pattern using size 3 (3mm) needles *or size necessary to obtain correct gauge.*

YARN NOTE

This garment was knitted originally in Rowan *4ply Cotton*. We suggest you substitute Rowan *Siena*, which knits to a very similar gauge. However, make sure you do a gauge swatch and, if necessary, adapt your needle size (up or down) to achieve the gauge on the pattern. If you do not, even a couple of stitches/rows difference on a thick yarn over a 4in/10cm swatch will make a noticeable difference to the width/length of the garment. For further information, see page 140.

BACK

Cast on 115 (123: 131: 139: 147) sts using size 1 (2.25mm) needles and yarn B.

Break off yarn B and join in yarn A.

Row 1 (RS): K1, *P1, K1, rep from * to end.

Row 2: P1, *K1, P1, rep from * to end.

Last 2 rows form rib.

Cont in rib, dec 1 st at each end of 13th and every foll 6th row until 103 (111: 119: 127: 135) sts rem.

Work a further 3 rows, ending with a WS row.

Change to size 3 (3mm) needles.

Row 1 (RS): K4, *K2tog tbl, [K1, yo] twice, K1, K2tog, K1, rep from * to last 3 sts, K3.

Row 2: P3, *P1, P2tog, [P1, yo] twice, P1, P2tog tbl, rep from * to last 4 sts, P4.

Row 3: K2tog, K2, *yo, K2tog tbl, K3, K2tog, yo, K1, rep from * to last 3 sts, K1, K2tog.
101 (109: 117: 125: 133) sts.

Row 4: P2, *P2, yo, P2tog, P1, P2tog tbl, yo, P1, rep from * to last 3 sts, P3.

Row 5: K3, *K2, yo, sk2p, yo, K3; rep from * to last 2 sts, K2.

Row 6: P2, *P1, P2tog, [P1, yo] twice, P1, P2tog tbl, rep from * to last 3 sts, P3.

Row 7: K3, *K2tog tbl, [K1, yo] twice, K1, K2tog, K1, rep from * to last 2 sts, K2.

Row 8: P2, *P1, yo, P2tog, P3, P2tog tbl, yo, rep from * to last 3 sts, P3.

Row 9: K2tog, K1, *K1, yo, K2tog tbl, K1, K2tog, yo, K2, rep from * to last 2 sts, K2tog.
99 (107: 115: 123: 131) sts.

Row 10: P1, *P3, yo, P3tog, yo, P2, rep from * to last 2 sts, P2.

These 10 rows form patt and cont side seam shaping.

Cont in patt, shaping side seams by inc 1 st at each end of 11th and every foll 10th row to 107 (115: 123: 131: 139) sts, then on every foll 8th row until there are 115 (123: 131: 139: 147) sts, taking inc sts into St st until there are sufficient to take into patt.

Cont even until back measures 14 (14$\frac{1}{2}$: 14$\frac{1}{2}$: 15: 15)in/36 (37: 37: 38: 38)cm, ending with a WS row.

Shape armholes

Keeping patt correct, bind off 5 (6: 6: 7: 7) sts at beg of next 2 rows. *105 (111: 119: 125: 133) sts.*

Dec 1 st at each end of next 5 (5: 7: 7: 9) rows, then on foll 3 (5: 5: 7: 7) alt rows. *89 (91: 95: 97: 101) sts.*

Cont even until armhole measures 7 (7: 7$\frac{1}{2}$: 7$\frac{1}{2}$: 8)in/18 (18: 19: 19: 20)cm, ending with a WS row.

Shape shoulders and back neck

Bind off 8 (8: 9: 9: 10) sts at beg of next 2 rows. *73 (75: 77: 79: 81) sts.*

Next row (RS): Bind off 8 (8: 9: 9: 10) sts, patt until there are 13 sts on right needle and turn, leaving rem sts on a holder.

Work each side of neck separately.

Bind off 4 sts at beg of next row. Bind off rem 9 sts. With RS facing, rejoin yarn to rem sts, bind off center 31 (33: 33: 35: 35) sts, patt to end.

Complete to match first side, reversing shapings.

FRONT

Work as given for back until 8 rows less have been worked than on back to beg of armhole shaping, ending with a WS row.

Divide for front opening

Next row (RS): Patt 54 (58: 62: 66: 70) sts and turn, leaving rem sts on a holder.

Work each side of neck separately.

Work 7 rows, ending with a WS row.

Shape armhole

Keeping patt correct, bind off 5 (6: 6: 7: 7) sts at beg of next row. *49 (52: 56: 59: 63) sts.*

Work 1 row.

Dec 1 st at armhole edge of next 5 (5: 7: 7: 9) rows, then on foll 3 (5: 5: 7: 7) alt rows. *41 (42: 44: 45: 47) sts.*

Cont even until 23 (23: 23: 25: 25) fewer rows have

been worked than on back to start of shoulder shaping, ending with a RS row.

Shape neck

Keeping patt correct, bind off 6 (7: 7: 7: 7) sts at beg of next row. *35 (35: 37: 38: 40) sts.*

Dec 1 st at neck edge of next 5 rows, then on foll 4 (4: 4: 5: 5) alt rows, then on foll 4th row. *25 (25: 27: 27: 29) sts.*

Work 5 rows, ending with a WS row.

Shape shoulder

Bind off 8 (8: 9: 9: 10) sts at beg of next and foll alt row.

Work 1 row.

Bind off rem 9 sts.

With RS facing, rejoin yarn to rem sts, bind off center 7 sts, patt to end.

Complete to match first side, reversing shapings.

SLEEVES (both alike)

Cast on 63 (63: 65: 67: 67) sts using size 1 (2.25mm) needles and yarn B.

Break off yarn B and join in yarn A.

Work in rib as given for back, shaping sides by inc 1 st at each end of 15th and foll 12th (10th: 10th: 10th: 10th) row, taking inc sts into rib. *67 (67: 69: 71: 71) sts.*

Work a further 5 (7: 7: 7: 7) rows, ending with a WS row.

Change to size 3 (3mm) needles.

Row 1 (RS): K2 (2: 3: 4: 4), *K2tog tbl, [K1, yo] twice, K1, K2tog, K1, rep from * to last 1 (1: 2: 3: 3) sts, K1 (1: 2: 3: 3).

Row 2: P1 (1: 2: 3: 3), *P1, P2tog, [P1, yo] twice, P1, P2tog tbl, rep from * to last 2 (2: 3: 4: 4) sts, P2 (2: 3: 4: 4).

Row 3: [Inc in first st] 0 (1: 1: 1: 1) times, K2 (1: 2: 3: 3), *yo, K2tog tbl, K3, K2tog, yo, K1, rep from * to last 1 (1: 2: 3: 3) sts, K1 (0: 1: 2: 2), [inc in last st] 0 (1: 1: 1: 1) times. *67 (69: 71: 73: 73) sts.*

Row 4: P1 (2: 3: 4: 4), *P2, yo, P2tog, P1, P2tog

Special tip

SHAPING THROUGH LACE

When working shaping within a lace pattern such as here, it is vitally important that each part pattern repeat at the ends of the rows is worked correctly. Here, the first full pattern repeat (of 10 rows) is explained so you know exactly how to work the shaping at the same time as the lacy pattern. From this point on, you need to ensure each lacy "hole" (increase) of the pattern is matched by a decrease on these part pattern repeats. You may find it easiest to place markers on the needle at each end of the full pattern repeats—at the * at the beginning of the row, and at the end of the last full pattern repeat at the end of the row. Between these markers, all stitches are worked in pattern. Beyond the markers, you will need to work the required shaping increase or decrease as well as keeping the pattern correct. Many knitters find it quite tricky to do this and prefer to work the edge stitches in stockinette stitch, rather than the pattern. For a lacy pattern such as this one, where the pattern repeat is just 8 stitches, this will not affect the finished look of the garment to any great extent. Whether you work the part pattern repeats in pattern or not, as the number of stitches increases or decreases, move the markers out or in by one full pattern repeat so you can keep track of exactly where each full pattern repeat begins and ends.

tbl, yo, P1, rep from * to last 2 (3: 4: 5: 5) sts, P2 (3: 4: 5: 5).

Row 5: [Inc in first st] 1 (0: 0: 0: 0) times, K1 (3: 4: 5: 5), *K2, yo, sk2p, yo, K3; rep from * to last 1 (2: 3: 4: 4) sts, K0 (2: 3: 4: 4), [inc in last st] 1 (0: 0: 0: 0) times. *69 (69: 71: 73: 73) sts.*

Row 6: P2 (2: 3: 4: 4), *P1, P2tog, [P1, yo] twice, P1, P2tog tbl, rep from * to last 3 (3: 4: 5: 5) sts, P3 (3: 4: 5: 5).

Row 7: K3 (3: 4: 5: 5), *K2tog tbl, [K1, yo] twice, K1, K2tog, K1, rep from * to last 2 (2: 3: 4: 4) sts, K2 (2: 3: 4: 4).

Row 8: P2 (2: 3: 4: 4), *P1, yo, P2tog, P3, P2tog tbl, yo, rep from * to last 3 (3: 4: 5: 5) sts, P3 (3: 4: 5: 5).

Row 9: K3 (3: 4: 5: 5), *K1, yo, K2tog tbl, K1, K2tog, yo, K2, rep from * to last 2 (2: 3: 4: 4) sts, K2 (2: 3: 4: 4).

Row 10: P2 (2: 3: 4: 4), *P3, yo, P3tog, yo, P2, rep from * to last 3 (3: 4: 5: 5) sts, P3 (3: 4: 5: 5).

These 10 rows form patt and cont side shaping.

Cont in patt, shaping side seams by inc 1 st at each end of 9th (3rd: 3rd: 3rd: 3rd) and every foll 12th (10th: 10th: 10th: 8th) row to 73 (91: 89: 91: 103) sts, then on every foll 10th (8th: 8th: 8th: -) row until there are 91 (93: 97: 99: -) sts, taking inc sts into St st until there are sufficient to take into patt.

Cont even until sleeve measures 17 (17: 17$\frac{1}{2}$: 17$\frac{1}{2}$: 17$\frac{1}{2}$)in/43 (43: 44: 44: 44)cm, ending with a WS row.

Shape top

Keeping patt correct, bind off 5 (6: 6: 7: 7) sts at beg of next 2 rows. *81 (81: 85: 85: 89) sts.*

Dec 1 st at each end of next 5 rows, then on foll 3 alt rows, then on every foll 4th row until 51 (51: 55: 55: 59) sts rem.

Work 1 row, ending with a WS row.

Dec 1 st at each end of next and every foll alt row to 45 sts, then on foll 5 rows, ending with a WS row.

Bind off rem 35 sts.

FINISHING

PRESS as described on the information page 138. Join shoulder seams using back stitch, or mattress stitch if preferred.

Button band

With RS facing, using size 1 (2.25mm) needles and yarn A, pick up and knit 41 (41: 43: 43: 45) sts down left front opening edge, between neck shaping and base of front opening.

Row 1 (WS): K1, *P1, K1, rep from * to end.

Row 2: K2, *P1, K1, rep from * to last st, K1.

These 2 rows form rib.

Work in rib for a further 7 rows, ending with a WS row.

Bind off in rib.

Buttonhole band

With RS facing, using size 1 (2.25mm) needles and yarn A, pick up and knit 41 (41: 43: 43: 45) sts up right front opening edge, between base of front opening and neck shaping.

Work in rib as given for button band for 4 rows.

Row 5 (WS): Rib 2, *work 2 tog, yo (to make a buttonhole), rib 6, rep from * 3 times more, work 2 tog, yo (to make 5th buttonhole), rib to end.

Work in rib for a further 4 rows.

Bind off in rib.

Collar

With RS facing, using size 1 (2.25mm) needles and yarn A, starting and ending halfway across top of bands, pick up and knit 37 (38: 38: 41: 41) sts up right side of neck, 39 (41: 41: 43: 43) sts from back, then 37 (38: 38: 41: 41) sts down left side of neck. *113 (117: 117: 125: 125) sts.*

Beg with row 2, work in rib as given for button band for 4 rows.

Row 5 (RS of collar, WS of body): K2, M1, rib to last 2 sts, M1, K2.

Row 6: K1, P1, rib to last 2 sts, P1, K1.

Rep last 2 rows 13 times more.

141 (145: 145: 153: 153) sts.

Work a further 2 rows.

Break off yarn A and join in yarn B.

Work 1 row.

Bind off in rib.

See information page 138 for finishing instructions, setting in sleeves using the set-in method. Lay button band over buttonhole band and stitch in place at base of front opening.

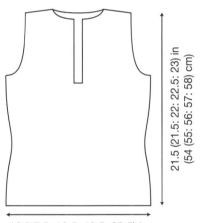

16 (17.5: 18.5: 19.5: 20.5) in
(41 (44: 47: 49.5: 52.5) cm)

21.5 (21.5: 22: 22.5: 23) in
(54 (55: 56: 57: 58) cm)

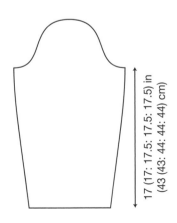

17 (17: 17.5: 17.5: 17.5) in
(43 (43: 44: 44: 44) cm)

Bay

Here you have two different versions of this delicate striped design in Rowan *Kidsilk Haze*, one with a warm and cozy polo neck and the other with a more summery boat neck. The stripe pattern is made up of a thick and thin stripe, with one shade of yarn used double and the other used single. The toning beaded hat, Pascale (see page 50), is knitted in a different yarn.

YARN AND SIZES

	XS	S	M	L	XL	
To fit bust	32	34	36	38	40	in
	81	86	91	97	102	cm

Lightweight (CYCA Fine) yarn
Rowan *Kidsilk Haze* (70% super kid mohair; 30% silk; 229yd/25g)

Polo neck sweater

		XS	S	M	L	XL	
A	Trance 582	5	5	5	6	6	balls
B	Meadow 581	3	3	3	3	3	balls

Crew neck sweater

		XS	S	M	L	XL	
A	Heavenly 592	4	4	4	4	4	balls
B	Hurricane 632	2	2	3	3	3	balls

(Crew neck sweater originally photographed in Pearl 590 and Nightly 585)

NEEDLES

1 pair size 3 (3.25mm) needles
1 pair size 5 (3.75mm) needles
1 pair size 6 (4mm) needles
1 pair size 7 (4.5mm) needles
2 double-pointed size 2 (2.75mm) needles

GAUGE

20 sts and 30 rows to 4in/10cm measured over striped stockinette stitch pattern using size 5 (3.75mm) and size 7 (4.5mm) needles and yarn A DOUBLE and yarn B SINGLE *or size necessary to obtain correct gauge.*

SPECIAL ABBREVIATIONS

Right dec = skp, slip st now on right needle back onto left needle, lift second st on left needle over first st and off left needle, then slip same st back onto right needle—2 sts decreased.
Left dec = sk2p—2 sts decreased.

Polo neck sweater

BACK

Cast on 88 (92: 98: 102: 108) sts using size 3 (3.25mm) needles and yarn A DOUBLE.

Work in garter st for 6 rows, ending with a WS row.

Join in yarn B SINGLE.

Beg with a K row, cont in striped St st patt as foll:

Using size 7 (4.5mm) needles and yarn B SINGLE, work 2 rows.

Using size 5 (3.75mm) needles and yarn A DOUBLE, work 2 rows.

These 4 rows form striped St st patt.

Work in patt for a further 10 rows, end with a WS row.

Keeping patt correct, cont as foll:

Place markers on 23rd (24th: 25th: 26th: 27th) st in from both ends of last row.

Next row (dec) (RS): K2tog, K to within 1 st of first marker, right dec, K to within 1 st of second marker, left dec, K to last 2 sts, K2tog.

Work 9 rows.

Rep last 10 rows once more, then first of these rows (the dec row) again. *70 (74: 80: 84: 90) sts.*

Work 19 rows, ending with a WS row.

Next row (inc) (RS): Inc in first st, [K to marked st, M1, K marked st, M1] twice, K to last st, inc in last st.

Work 13 rows.

Rep last 14 rows once more, then first of these rows (the inc row) again. *88 (92: 98: 102: 108) sts.*

Cont even until back measures 13³/₄ (14: 14: 14¹/₂: 14¹/₂)in/35 (36: 36: 37: 37)cm, ending with a WS row.

Shape armholes

Keeping patt correct, bind off 3 (4: 4: 5: 5) sts at beg of next 2 rows. *82 (84: 90: 92: 98) sts.*

Dec 1 st at each end of next 5 (5: 7: 7: 9) rows, then on foll 3 alt rows. *66 (68: 70: 72: 74) sts.*

Cont even until armhole measures 8 (8: 8¹/₄:8¹/₄: 8³/₄)in/20 (20: 21: 21: 22)cm, ending with a WS row.

Shape shoulders and back neck

Bind off 5 (5: 5: 5: 6) sts at beg of next 2 rows. *56 (58: 60: 62: 62) sts.*

Next row (RS): Bind off 5 (5: 5: 5: 6) sts, K until there are 9 (9: 10: 10: 9) sts on right needle and turn, leaving rem sts on a holder.

Work each side of neck separately.

Bind off 4 sts at beg of next row.

Bind off rem 5 (5: 6: 6: 5) sts.

With RS facing, rejoin yarns to rem sts, bind off center 28 (30: 30: 32: 32) sts, K to end.

Complete to match first side, reversing shapings.

FRONT

Work as given for back until 18 (18: 18: 20: 20)

rows less have been worked than on back to start of shoulder shaping, ending with a WS row.

Shape neck

Next row (RS): K24 (24: 25: 26: 27) and turn, leaving rem sts on a holder.

Work each side of neck separately.

Dec 1 st at neck edge of next 5 rows, then on foll 3 (3: 3: 4: 4) alt rows, then on foll 4th row. *15 (15: 16: 16: 17) sts.*

Work 2 rows, ending with a WS row.

Shape shoulder

Bind off 5 (5: 5: 5: 6) sts at beg of next and foll alt row.

Work 1 row. Bind off rem 5 (5: 6: 6: 5) sts.

With RS facing, rejoin yarns to rem sts, bind off center 18 (20: 20: 20: 20) sts, K to end.

Complete to match first side, reversing shapings.

SLEEVES (both alike)

Cast on 64 (66: 68: 70: 72) sts using size 3 (3.25mm) needles and yarn A DOUBLE.

Work in garter st for 2 rows, ending with a WS row.

Row 3 (eyelet row) (RS): K1, *K2tog, yo, rep from * to last st, K1.

Work in garter st for a further 3 rows, ending with a WS row.

Join in yarn B SINGLE and cont in striped St st patt as given for back until sleeve measures 19³/₄ (19³/₄: 20: 20: 20)in/50 (50: 51: 51: 51)cm, ending with a WS row.

Shape top

Keeping patt correct, bind off 3 (4: 4: 5: 5) sts at beg of next 2 rows. *58 (58: 60: 60: 62) sts.*

Dec 1 st at each end of next 3 rows, then on foll 2 alt rows, then on every foll 4th row until 36 (36: 38: 38: 40) sts rem.

Work 1 row, ending with a WS row.

Dec 1 st at each end of next and every foll alt row to 32 sts, then on foll 5 rows, ending with a WS

row.

Bind off rem 22 sts.

FINISHING

PRESS as described on the information page 138.

Join right shoulder seam using back stitch, or mattress stitch if preferred.

Collar

With RS facing, using size 3 (3.25mm) needles and yarn A DOUBLE, pick up and knit 22 (22: 22: 24: 24) sts down left side of neck, 18 (20: 20: 20: 20) sts from front, 22 (22: 22: 24: 24) sts up right side of neck, then 36 (38: 38: 40: 40) sts from back.

98 (102: 102: 108: 108) sts.

Beg with a K row, work in striped St st as foll:

Using size 3 (3.25mm) needles and yarn A DOUBLE, work 2 rows.

Using size 6 (4mm) needles and yarn B SINGLE, work 2 rows.

Rep last 4 rows 7 times more.

Using size 5 (3.75mm) needles and yarn A DOUBLE, work 2 rows.

Using size 7 (4.5mm) needles and yarn B SINGLE, work 2 rows.

These 4 rows form striped St st patt.

Cont in patt until collar measures 10in/25cm, ending with 2 rows using yarn B.

Using size 5 (3.75mm) needles, yarn A DOUBLE and beg with a P row, work in rev St st for 3 rows.

Bind off loosely knitwise.

See information page 138 for finishing instructions, setting in sleeves using the set-in method.

Ties (make 2)

With double-pointed size 2 (2.75mm) needles and yarn A SINGLE, cast on 4 sts.

Row 1 (RS): K4, *without turning work slip these 4 sts to opposite end of needle and bring yarn to opposite end of work pulling it quite tightly across back of these 4 sts, using other needle K these 4 sts again; rep from * until tie is 17³/₄in/45cm long, K4tog and fasten off.

Thread ties through eyelet holes around each cuff.

Crew neck sweater

BACK and FRONT

Work as for back and front of polo neck sweater.

SLEEVES (both alike)

Cast on 42 (42: 44: 46: 46) sts using size 3 (3.25mm) needles and yarn A DOUBLE.

Work in garter st for 6 rows, ending with a WS row.

Join in yarn B SINGLE and cont in striped St st patt as given for back, shaping sides by inc 1 st at each end of 25th and every foll 8th (6th: 8th: 8th: 6th) row to 60 (48: 68: 70: 56) sts, then on every foll 10th (8th: -: -: 8th) row until there are 64 (66: -: -: 72) sts.

Cont even until sleeve measures 17 (17: 17¹/₂: 17¹/₂: 17¹/₂)in/43 (43: 44: 44: 44)cm, ending with a WS row.

Shape top

Keeping patt correct, bind off 3 (4: 4: 5: 5) sts at beg of next 2 rows. *58 (58: 60: 60: 62) sts.*

Dec 1 st at each end of next 3 rows, then on foll 2 alt rows, then on every foll 4th row until 36 (36: 38: 38: 40) sts rem.

Work 1 row, ending with a WS row.

Dec 1 st at each end of next and every foll alt row to 32 sts, then on foll 5 rows, ending with a WS row.

Bind off rem 22 sts.

FINISHING

PRESS as described on the information page 138.

Join right shoulder seam using back stitch, or mattress stitch if preferred.

Neckband

With RS facing, using size 3 (3.25mm) needles and yarn A DOUBLE, pick up and knit 22 (22: 22: 24: 24) sts down left side of neck, 18 (20: 20: 20: 20) sts from front, 22 (22: 22: 24: 24) sts up right side of neck, then 36 (38: 38: 40: 40) sts from back. *98 (102: 102: 108: 108) sts.*

Row 1 (WS): Knit.

Row 2 (eyelet row): K1, *K2tog, yo, rep from * to last st, K1.

Work in garter st for 2 rows.

Bind off loosely knitwise (on WS).

See information page 138 for finishing instructions, setting in sleeves using the set-in method.

Tie

With double-pointed size 2 (2.75mm) needles and yarn B SINGLE, cast on 4 sts.

Row 1 (RS): K4, *without turning work slip these 4 sts to opposite end of needle and bring yarn to opposite end of work pulling it quite tightly across back of these 4 sts, using other needle K these 4 sts again; rep from * until tie is 37¹/₂in/95cm long, K4tog and fasten off.

Thread tie through eyelet holes around neckband.

21.5 (22: 22.5: 23: 23) in
(55 (56: 57: 58: 59) cm)

17.5 (18: 19.5: 20: 21.5) in
(44 (46: 49: 51: 54) cm)

19.5 (19.5: 20: 20: 20) in
(50 (50: 51: 51: 51) cm)

17 (17: 17.5: 17.5: 17.5) in
(43 (43: 44: 44: 44) cm)

Pascale

YARN AND SIZES
One size, to fit average size adult head
Sport (CYCA Fine) yarn
Rowan *Fine Heritage Tweed* (100% wool; 98yd/25g) in Skipton 379
         3 balls
(Originally photographed in Rowan *Yorkshire Tweed 4ply* in Enchant 268)

NEEDLES
1 pair size 2 (2.75mm) needles
1 pair size 3 (3.25mm) needles

EXTRAS
Approx 1,300 x Rowan 01006 beads

GAUGE
26 sts and 38 rows to 4in/10cm measured over stockinette stitch using size 3 (3.25mm) needles *or size necessary to obtain correct gauge.*

YARN NOTE
This garment was knitted originally in Rowan *Yorkshire Tweed 4ply*. We suggest you substitute Rowan *Fine Heritage Tweed*, which knits to a very similar gauge. However, make sure you do a gauge swatch and, if necessary, adapt your needle size (up or down) to achieve the gauge on the pattern. If you do not, even a couple of stitches/rows difference on a thick yarn over a 4in/10cm swatch will make a noticeable difference to the width/length of the garment. For further information, see page 140.

BERET

Cast on 146 sts using size 2 (2.75mm) needles.

Row 1 (RS): K2, *P2, K2, rep from * to end.

Row 2: P2, *K2, P2, rep from * to end.

These 2 rows form rib.

Cont in rib for a further 7 rows, end with a RS row.

Row 10 (inc) (WS): Rib 2, *M1, rib 2, rep from * to end. *218 sts.*

Change to size 3 (3.25mm) needles.

Row 1 (RS): K2, *bead 1, K5, rep from * to end.

Row 2 and every foll alt row: Purl.

Row 3: K1, bead 1, *K1, bead 1, K3, bead 1, rep from * to last 6 sts, K1, bead 1, K4.

Row 5: K4, *bead 1, K1, bead 1, K3, rep from * to last 4 sts, [bead 1, K1] twice.

Row 7: *K5, bead 1, rep from * to last 2 sts, K2.

Row 9: Knit.

Row 11: As row 1.

Row 13: As row 3.

Row 15: As row 5.

Row 17: As row 7.

Row 19: As row 5.

Row 21: As row 3.

Row 23: As row 1.

Rows 25 and 27: Knit.

Row 29: [K9, K3tog] 18 times, K2. *182 sts.*

Row 31: *K1, bead 1, rep from * to last 2 sts, K2.

Row 33: Knit.

Row 35: K2, *bead 1, K1, rep from * to end.

Row 37: Knit.

Row 39: As row 31.

Row 41: Knit.

Row 43: K1, *[K1, bead 1] 3 times, K3tog, bead 1, rep from * to last st, K1. *146 sts.*

Row 45: Knit.

Row 47: As row 31.

Row 49: [K5, K3tog] 18 times, K2. *110 sts.*

Row 51: As row 35.

Row 53: [K3, K3tog] 18 times, K2. *74 sts.*

Row 55: As row 31.

Row 57: [K2, K2tog] 18 times, K2. *56 sts.*

Row 59: [K1, K2tog] 18 times, K2. *38 sts.*

Row 61: [K2tog] 19 times.

Row 62: Purl.

Break yarn and thread through rem 19 sts. Pull up tight and fasten off securely.

FINISHING

Join back seam using back stitch, or mattress stitch if preferred. Cut a 10½in/27cm diameter circle of card and slip inside beret. **PRESS** as described on the information page 138.

SPECIAL ABBREVIATIONS

Bead 1 = place a bead by bringing yarn to front (RS) of work and slipping bead up next to st just worked, slip next st purlwise from left needle to right needle and take yarn back to back (WS) of work, leaving bead sitting in front of slipped st on RS.

Beading note: Before starting to knit, thread beads onto yarn. To do this, thread a fine sewing needle (one that will easily pass through the beads) with sewing thread. Knot ends of thread and then pass end of yarn through this loop. Thread a bead onto sewing thread and then gently slide it along and onto knitting yarn. Continue in this way until required number of beads are on yarn.

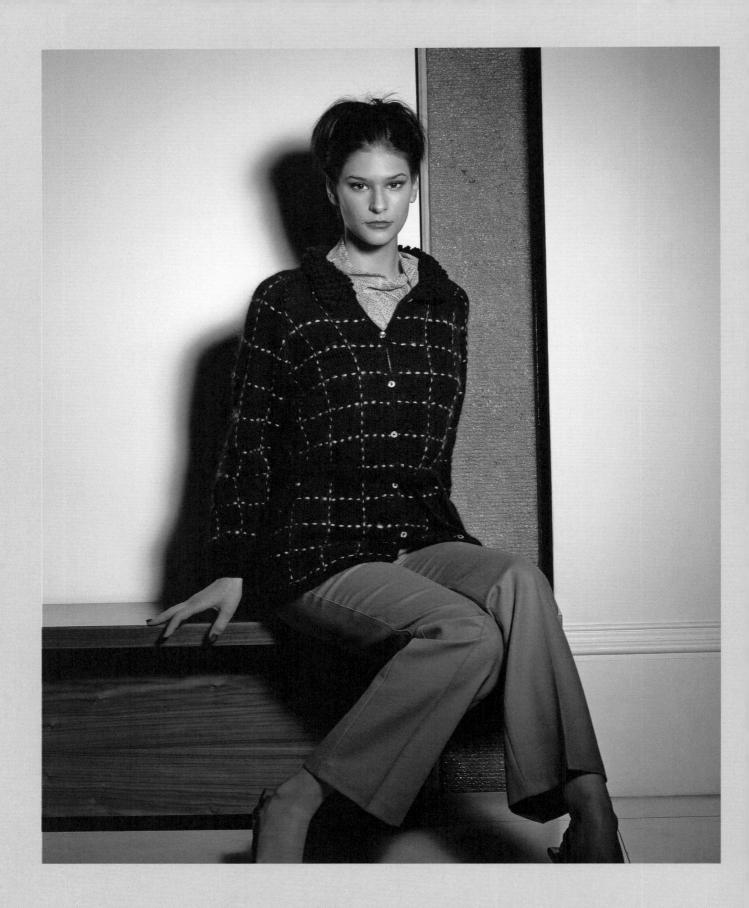

Woo

An elegant combination of cardigan and sweater patterns, knitted in Rowan *Kid Classic*, a very soft yet warm yarn with a lofty feel. It comes in both women's and children's sizes. You can choose to embroider the cardigan with a checkerboard design in large running stitches, using *Kidsilk Haze*, and it also has an optional knitted belt. The sweater is long line with a deep cowl neck.

YARN AND SIZES

To fit age	6–7	8–9	10–11	12–13		years

	XS	S	M	L	XL	
To fit bust	32	34	36	38	40	in
	81	86	91	97	102	cm

Worsted (CYCA Medium) yarn
Rowan *Kid Classic* (70% lambswool, 25% kid mohair, 4% nylon; 153yd/50g)
Children's in Bear 817

Jacket	7	8	9	9		balls
Sweater	6	7	8	9		balls

(Originally photographed in Imp 829)
Ladies'
Jacket in Peat 832

	10	10	11	11	12	balls

Sweater in Feather 828

	9	10	10	11	11	balls

Embroidered version only: 1 ball of *Kidsilk Haze* in Straw 851 (originally photographed in Toffee 598)

NEEDLES
1 pair size 6 (4mm) needles
1 pair size 8 (5mm) needles

EXTRAS
Buttons: 7 for jacket

GAUGE
19 sts and 25 rows to 4in/10cm measured over stockinette stitch using size 8 (5mm) needles *or size necessary to obtain correct gauge.*

Pattern note: The pattern is written for the 4 children's sizes, followed by the ladies' sizes in **bold**. Where only one figure appears this applies to all sizes in that group.

Jacket

BACK

Cast on 75 (81: 85: 91: **95: 101: 105: 111: 115**) sts using size 6 (4mm) needles.

Work in garter st for 6 rows, ending with a WS row.

Change to size 8 (5mm) needles.

Next row (RS): K1 (4: 6: 9: **11: 2: 4: 7: 9**), *P1, K11, rep from * to last 2 (5: 7: 10: **12: 3: 5: 8: 10**) sts, P1, K1 (4: 6: 9: **11: 2: 4: 7: 9**).

This row sets position of optional embroidered vertical stripes.

Beg with a P row, cont in St st as foll:

Work 19 (21: 23: 25: **27) rows, end with a WS row.

Dec 1 st at each end of next and every foll 10th (10th: 8th: 8th: **8th**) row until there are 65 (71: 73: 79: **87: 93: 97: 103: 107**) sts, then on every foll - (**6th**) row until there are - (**81: 87: 91: 97: 101**) sts.

Work 7 (9: 9: 9: **9**) rows, ending with a WS row.

Inc 1 st at each end of next and every foll 6th row until there are 71 (77: 81: 87: **87: 93: 97: 103: 107**) sts, then on every foll 4th row until there are 75 (81: 85: 91: **95: 101: 105: 111: 115**) sts.***

Cont even until back measures 15³/₄ (16¹/₂ :17¹/₄: 18: **19**)in/40 (42: 44: 46: **48**) cm, ending with a WS row.

Shape raglan armholes

Bind off 3 (**5**) sts at beg of next 2 rows.

*69 (75: 79: 85: **85: 91: 95: 101: 105**) sts.*

Next row (RS): P2, K3tog, K to last 5 sts, K3tog tbl, P2.

Next row: K2, P to last 2 sts, K2.

Rep last 2 rows 2 (3: 4: 5: **4: 5: 6: 7: 8**) times more.

*57 (59: 59: 61: **65: 67: 67: 69: 69**) sts.*

Next row (RS): P2, K3tog, K to last 5 sts, K3tog tbl, P2.

Next row: K2, P to last 2 sts, K2.

Next row: P2, K to last 2 sts, P2.

Next row: K2, P to last 2 sts, K2.****

Rep last 4 rows 9 (**10**) times more.

Bind off rem 17 (19: 19: 21: **21: 23: 23: 25: 25**) sts.

LEFT FRONT

Cast on 38 (41: 43: 46: **48: 51: 53: 56: 58**) sts using size 6 (4mm) needles.

Work in garter st for 6 rows, ending with a WS row.

Change to size 8 (5mm) needles.

Next row (RS): K1 (4: 6: 9: **11: 2: 4: 7: 9**), *P1, K11, rep from * to last st, K1.

This row sets position of embroidered vertical stripes.

Beg with a P row, cont in St st as foll:

Work 19 (21: 23: 25: **27**) rows, ending with a WS row.

Dec 1 st at beg of next and every foll 10th (10th: 8th: 8th: **8th**) row until there are 33 (36: 37: 40: **44: 47: 49: 52: 54**) sts, then on every foll - (**6th**) row until there are - (**41: 44: 46: 49: 51**) sts.

Work 7 (9: 9: 9: **9**) rows, ending with a WS row.

Inc 1 st at beg of next and every foll 6th row until there are 36 (39: 41: 44: **44: 47: 49: 52: 54**) sts, then on every foll 4th row until there are 38 (41: 43: 46: **48: 51: 53: 56: 58**) sts.

Cont even until left front matches back to beg of raglan armhole shaping, ending with a WS row.

Shape raglan armhole

Bind off 3 (**5**) sts at beg of next row.

*35 (38: 40: 43: **43: 46: 48: 51: 53**) sts.*

Work 1 row.

Next row (RS): P2, K3tog, K to end.

Next row: P to last 2 sts, K2.

Rep last 2 rows 2 (3: 4: 5: **4: 5: 6: 7: 8**) times more.

*29 (30: 30: 31: **33: 34: 34: 35: 35**) sts.*

Next row (RS): P2, K3tog, K to end.

Next row: P to last 2 sts, K2.

Next row: P2, K to end.

Next row: P to last 2 sts, K2.

Rep last 4 rows 5 (5: 4: 4: **5: 5: 5: 4: 4**) times more.

*17 (18: 20: 21: **21: 22: 22: 25: 25**) sts.*

Working all raglan decreases 2 sts in from raglan

edge and keeping sts correct as now set, cont as foll:

Dec 2 sts at raglan edge of next row.

*15 (16: 18: 19: **19: 20: 20: 23: 23**) sts.*

Work 0 (0: 2: 2: **0: 0: 0: 2: 2**) rows, end with a RS row.

Shape neck

Bind off 6 (7: 6: 7: **7: 8: 8: 8: 8**) sts at beg of next row. *9 (9: 12: 12: **12: 12: 12: 15: 15**) sts.*

Dec 1 st at neck edge of next 3 rows, then on foll 1 (1: 2: 2: **1: 1: 1: 2: 2**) alt rows **and at same time** dec 2 sts at raglan edge on every foll 4th row from previous dec. *3 (6) sts.*

Ladies' sizes only

Work 1 row.

Dec 2 sts at raglan edge of next row. *4 sts.*

Work 1 row.

Dec 1 st at neck edge of next row. *3 sts.*

All sizes

Work 1 row.

Dec 2 sts at raglan edge of next row.

Next row (WS): K1 and fasten off.

RIGHT FRONT

Cast on 38 (41: 43: 46: **48: 51: 53: 56: 58**) sts using size 6 (4mm) needles.

Work in garter st for 6 rows, ending with a WS row.

Change to size 8 (5mm) needles.

Next row (RS): K1, *K11, P1, rep from * to last 1 (4: 6: 9: **11: 2: 4: 7: 9**) sts, K1 (4: 6: 9: **11: 2: 4: 7: 9**).

This row sets position of embroidered vertical stripes.

Beg with a P row, cont in St st as foll:

Work 19 (21: 23: 25: **27**) rows, ending with a WS row.

Dec 1 st at end of next and every foll 10th (10th: 8th: 8th: **8th**) row until there are 33 (36: 37: 40: **44: 47: 49: 52: 54**) sts, then on every foll - (**6th**) row until there are - (**41: 44: 46: 49: 51**) sts.

Complete to match left front, reversing shapings.

SLEEVES
Cast on 39 (41: 43: 45: **47: 47: 49: 51: 51**) sts using size 6 (4mm) needles.
Row 1 (RS): K7 (8: 9: 10: **11: 11: 0: 1: 1**), *P1, K11, rep from * to last 8 (9: 10: 11: **12: 12: 1: 2: 2**), P1, K7 (8: 9: 10: **11: 11: 0: 1: 1**).
This row sets position of embroidered vertical stripes.
Beg with a P row, work in St st for 5 rows, ending with a WS row.
Change to size 8 (5mm) needles.
Cont in St st, shaping sides by inc 1 st at each end of next and every foll 6th row to 49 (55: 65: 71: **79: 71: 75: 73: 69**) sts, then on every foll 4th row until there are 71 (75: 77: 81: **83: 87: 89: 93: 95**) sts.
Cont even until sleeve measures $13^1/_2$ ($14^1/_2$: $15^3/_4$: 17: **18: 18: $18^1/_2$: $18^1/_2$**)in/34 (37: 40: 43: **46: 46: 47: 47: 47**)cm, ending with a WS row.
Shape raglan
Bind off 3 (**5**) sts at beg of next 2 rows.
*65 (69: 71: 75: **73: 77: 79: 83: 85**) sts.*
Next row (RS): P2, K3tog, K to last 5 sts, K3tog tbl, P2.
Next row: K2, P to last 2 sts, K2.
Rep last 2 rows 4 (5: 4: 5: **2: 3: 2: 3: 2**) times more.
*45 (45: 51: 51: **61: 61: 67: 67: 73**) sts.*
Next row (RS): P2, K3tog, K to last 5 sts, K3tog tbl, P2.
Next row: K2, P to last 2 sts, K2.
Next row: P2, K to last 2 sts, P2.
Next row: K2, P to last 2 sts, K2.
Rep last 4 rows 6 (6: 7: 7: **9: 9: 10: 10: 11**) times more and then first 2 rows again.
*13 (13: 15: 15: **17: 17: 19: 19: 21**) sts.*
Working all raglan decreases 2 sts in from raglan edge and keeping sts correct as now set, cont as foll:
Left sleeve only

Work 1 row.

Bind off 3 (**4: 4: 4: 4: 5**) sts at beg of next row. *10 (10: 12: 12: **13: 13: 15: 15: 16**) sts.*

Next row (RS): P2, K3tog, K to end. *8 (8: 10: 10: **11: 11: 13: 13: 14**) sts.*

Bind off 3 (**4: 4: 4: 4: 5**) sts at beg of next row. *5 (5: 7: 7: **7: 7: 9: 9: 9**) sts.*

Work 1 row.

Bind off 3 (**4: 4: 4: 4: 5**) sts at beg of next row.

Right sleeve only

Bind off 3 (**4: 4: 4: 4: 5**) sts at beg of next row. *10 (10: 12: 12: **13: 13: 15: 15: 16**) sts.*

Work 1 row.

Next row (RS): Bind off 3 (**4: 4: 4: 4: 5**) sts, K to last 5 sts, K3tog tbl, P2. *5 (5: 7: 7: **7: 7: 9: 9: 9**) sts.*

Work 1 row.

Bind off 3 (**4: 4: 4: 4: 5**) sts at beg of next row.

Work 1 row.

Both sleeves

Bind off rem 2 (2: 4: 4: **3: 3: 5: 5: 4**) sts.

Sweater

BACK

Work as given for back of jacket to ****, omitting side seam shaping from ** to ***.

Rep last 4 rows 7 (**8**) times more, and then first 2 rows again.

Bind off rem 21 (23: 23: 25: **25: 27: 27: 29: 29**) sts.

FRONT

Work as given for back until 37 (39: 39: 41: **45: 47: 47: 49: 49**) sts rem in raglan shaping.

Work 3 (3: 1: 1: **3: 3: 3: 1: 1**) rows, ending with a WS row.

Shape neck

Next row (RS): P2, [K3tog] 1 (1: 0: 0: **1: 1: 1: 0: 0**) times, K7 (7: 11: 11: **10: 10: 10: 14: 14**) and turn, leaving rem sts on a holder.

Working all raglan decreases 2 sts in from raglan edge and keeping sts correct as now set, work

each side of neck separately as foll:

Dec 1 st at neck edge on next 4 rows, then on foll 1 (1: 2: 2: **1: 1: 1: 2: 2**) alt rows **and at same time** dec 2 sts at raglan edge on every foll 4th row from previous dec. *3 (**6**) sts.*

Ladies' sizes only

Work 1 row.

Dec 2 sts at raglan edge on next row.

Work 1 row.

Dec 1 st at neck edge on next row. *3 sts.*

All sizes

Work 1 row.

Dec 2 sts at raglan edge on next row.

Next row (WS): K1 and fasten off.

With RS facing, rejoin yarn to rem sts and cont as foll:

Next row (RS): Bind off 13 (15: 13: 15: 17: 17: 17: 17) sts, K to last 5 (5: 2: 2: **5: 5: 2: 2**) sts, [K3tog tbl] 1 (1: 0: 0: **1: 1: 1: 0: 0**) times, P2.

Complete to match first side, reversing shapings.

SLEEVES

Work as given for sleeves of jacket until 17 (17: 19: 19: **21: 21: 23: 23: 25**) sts rem in raglan shaping.

Working all raglan decreases 2 sts in from raglan edge and keeping sts correct as now set, cont as foll:

Work 1 row, ending with a WS row.

Left sleeve only

Work 1 row.

Bind off 5 (5: 6: 6: **6: 6: 7: 7: 8**) sts at beg of next row. *12 (12: 13: 13: **15: 15: 16: 16: 17**) sts.*

Next row (RS): P2, K3tog, K to end. *10 (10: 11: 11: **13: 13: 14: 14: 15**) sts.*

Bind off 5 (5: 6: 6: **6: 6: 7: 7: 8**) sts at beg of next row. *5 (5: 5: 5: **7: 7: 7: 7: 7**) sts.*

Right sleeve only

Bind off 5 (5: 6: 6: **6: 6: 7: 7: 8**) sts at beg of next row. *12 (12: 13: 13: **15: 15: 16: 16: 17**) sts.*

Work 1 row.
Next row (RS): Bind off 5 (5: 6: 6: **6: 6: 7: 7: 8**) sts, K to last 5 sts, K3tog tbl, P2.
*5 (5: 5: 5: **7: 7: 7: 7: 7**) sts.*
Work 1 row.
Both sleeves
Bind off rem 5 (5: 5: 5: **7: 7: 7: 7: 7**) sts.

FINISHING
PRESS all pieces as described on the information page 138.
Optional embroidered version
Using photograph as a guide and using 4 strands of *Kidsilk Haze* held together, embroider vertical lines of running stitch from each purl stitch on marker rows of front(s), back, and sleeves. Work horizontal lines of running stitch in the same way on row 4 and every foll 14th row.
All versions
Join raglan seams using back stitch or mattress stitch.
Cuffs (both alike)
Cast on 39 (41: 43: 45: **47: 47: 49: 51: 51**) sts using size 8 (5mm) needles.
Work fringe trim as foll:
Row 1 (RS): K1, *cast on 4 sts then bind off the same 4 sts—one st more now on right needle (this will now be called "fringe 1"), K1, rep from * to end.
Row 2: K1, *P1, K1, rep from * to end.
Row 3: K2, *fringe 1, K1, rep from * to last st, K1.
Row 4: As row 2.
These 4 rows form fringe trim patt.
Rows 5 and 6: As rows 1 and 2.
Beg with a K row, cont in St st until cuff measures 2$\frac{1}{2}$ (**3**)in/6 (**7.5**)cm from cast-on edge. Bind off.
With RS of cuff against WS of sleeve, sew bound-off edge of cuff to sleeve. Turn to RS and catch in place.
Jacket
Button border
With RS facing and size 6 (4mm) needles, pick up and knit 100 (106: 112: 118: **118: 118: 124: 124: 124**) sts evenly along left front opening edge, between neck shaping and cast-on edge.
Knit 2 rows. Bind off knitwise (on WS).
Buttonhole border
Work as given for button border, picking up

sts along right front opening edge and making buttonholes in row 2 as foll:

Row 2 (RS): K5, *yo, K2tog, K13 (14: 15: 16: **16: 16: 17: 17: 17**), rep from * to last 5 sts, yo, K2tog, K3.

Collar

Cast on 63 (67: 73: 77: **85: 89: 93: 99: 103**) sts using size 8 (5mm) needles.

Beg with row 1, work in fringe trim patt as given for cuffs for 12 (**16**) rows. Bind off. Sew bound-off edge of collar in place, easing in fullness.

Belt

Using size 6 (4mm) needles, cast on 294 sts. Beg with a RS row, work 8 rows in garter st. Bind off knitwise (on WS).

Sweater
Collar

Cast on 79 (83: 89: 93: **101: 105: 109: 115: 119**) sts using size 8 (5mm) needles.

Work 6 rows of fringe trim as given for cuffs.

Beg with a K row, cont in St st until collar measures 5½ (**6¼**)in/14 (**16**)cm from cast-on edge.

Change to size 6 (4mm) needles.

Cont in St st until collar measures 8¾ (**10¼**)in/22 (**26**)cm from cast-on edge. Bind off. With RS facing, join row-end edges of collar to form tube. Sew bound-off edge of collar in place, easing in fullness.

See information page 138 for finishing instructions.

23 (24.5: 25.5: 27: **27.5: 28: 28.5: 28.5: 29**) in (59 (62: 65: 68: **70: 71: 72: 73: 74**) cm)

15.5 (16.5: 17.5: 19: **19.5: 21: 22: 23: 24**) in (39.5 (42.5: 44.5: 48: **50: 53: 55.5: 58.5: 60.5**) cm)

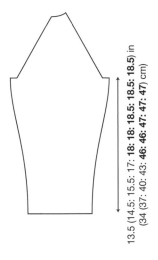

13.5 (14.5: 15.5: 17: **18: 18: 18.5: 18.5: 18.5**) in (34 (37: 40: 43: **46: 46: 47: 47: 47**) cm)

Asta

This elegant edge-to-edge summer cardigan knitted in *Cotton Glace* has a deep broadly ribbed welt and cuffs, finished with a ridged detail. The body of the cardigan has a textured pattern in an interesting openwork design, with little holes created in a lattice pattern. A broad satin ribbon is attached to each side of the cardigan fronts just above the welt.

YARN AND SIZES

	XS	S	M	L	XL	
To fit bust	32	34	36	38	40	in
	81	86	91	97	102	cm

Lightweight (CYCA Light) yarn
Rowan *Cotton Glace* (100% cotton; 126yd/50g)
in Garnet 841

	9	10	11	11	12	balls

(Originally photographed in Excite 815)

NEEDLES
1 pair size 2 (3mm) needles
1 pair size 3 (3.25mm) needles
Size 2 (3mm) circular needle

EXTRAS
35$\frac{1}{2}$in/90cm of 1$\frac{1}{4}$in/3.5cm wide double satin ribbon

GAUGE
23 sts and 32 rows to 4in/10cm measured over stockinette stitch using size 3 (3.25mm) needles *or size necessary to obtain correct gauge.*

BACK

Lower section

Cast on 96 (102: 108: 114: 120) sts using size 2 (3mm) needles.

Row 1 (RS): P0 (0: 1: 0: 0), K1 (0: 2: 2: 1), [P2, K2] 2 (3: 3: 4: 5) times, [P4, K3] twice, P2, [K3, P4] twice, [K3, P2] 3 times, [K3, P4] twice, K3, P2, [K3, P4] twice, [K2, P2] 2 (3: 3: 4: 5) times, K1 (0: 2: 2: 1), P0 (0: 1: 0: 0).

Row 2: K0 (0: 1: 0: 0), P1 (0: 2: 2: 1), [K2, P2] 2 (3: 3: 4: 5) times, [K4, P3] twice, K2, [P3, K4] twice, [P3, K2] 3 times, [P3, K4] twice, P3, K2, [P3, K4] twice, [P2, K2] 2 (3: 3: 4: 5) times, P1 (0: 2: 2: 1), K0 (0: 1: 0: 0).

These 2 rows form rib.

Work in rib for a further 8 rows, ending with a WS row.

Change to size 3 (3.25mm) needles.

Work in rib for a further 10 rows, ending with a WS row.

Row 21 (RS): Rib 11 (14: 17: 20: 23), P2tog, K3, P2tog, rib 12, P2tog, K3, P2tog, rib 22, P2tog, K3, P2tog, rib 12, P2tog, K3, P2tog, rib to end. *88 (94: 100: 106: 112) sts.*

Keeping rib correct as set, work 19 rows, ending with a WS row.

Row 41 (RS): Rib 10 (13: 16: 19: 22), P2tog, K3, P2tog, rib 10, P2tog, K3, P2tog, rib 20, P2tog, K3, P2tog, rib 10, P2tog, K3, P2tog, rib to end. *80 (86: 92: 98: 104) sts.*

Keeping rib correct as set, work 15 rows, ending with a WS row.

Bind off knitwise.

Upper section

With **WS** facing (so that ridge is formed on RS of work) and using size 3 (3.25mm) needles, pick up and knit 81 (87: 93: 99: 105) sts across bound-off edge of lower section.

Beg with a K row, work in St st for 4 rows, ending with a WS row.

Patt as foll:

Row 1 (RS): K3 (0: 3: 0: 3), *K2tog, yo, K4, rep from * to last 6 (3: 6: 3: 6) sts, K2tog, yo, K4 (1: 4: 1: 4).

Beg with a P row, work in St st for 7 rows, inc 1 st at each end of 2nd of these rows and ending with a WS row. *83 (89: 95: 101: 107) sts.*

Row 9 (RS): Inc in first st, K0 (3: 0: 3: 0), *K2tog, yo, K4, rep from * to last 4 (7: 4: 7: 4) sts, K2tog, yo, K1 (4: 1: 4: 1), inc in last st. *85 (91: 97: 103: 109) sts.*

Beg with a P row, work in St st for 7 rows, inc 1 st at each end of 6th of these rows and ending with a WS row. *87 (93: 99: 105: 111) sts.*

Last 16 rows form patt and start side seam shaping.

Cont in patt, shaping side seams by inc 1 st at each end of 5th and every foll 6th row until there are 97 (103: 109: 115: 121) sts, taking inc sts into patt.

Work 13 (15: 15: 17: 17) rows, ending with a WS row. (Back should measure 14 1/4 (14 1/2: 14 1/2: 15: 15)in/36 (37: 37: 38: 38)cm from cast-on edge of lower section.)

Shape armholes

Keeping patt correct, bind off 3 (4: 4: 5: 5) sts at beg of next 2 rows. *91 (95: 101: 105: 111) sts.*

Dec 1 st at each end of next 5 (5: 7: 7: 9) rows, then on foll 4 (5: 5: 6: 6) alt rows. *73 (75: 77: 79: 81) sts.*

Cont even until armhole measures 8 (8: 8 1/4: 8 1/4: 8 3/4)in/20 (20: 21: 21: 22)cm, ending with a WS row.

Shape shoulders and back neck

Bind off 7 (7: 7: 7: 8) sts at beg of next 2 rows. *59 (61: 63: 65: 65) sts.*

Next row (RS): Bind off 7 (7: 7: 7: 8) sts, patt until there are 11 (11: 12: 12: 11) sts on right needle and turn, leaving rem sts on a holder.

Work each side of neck separately.

Bind off 4 sts at beg of next row.
Bind off rem 7 (7: 8: 8: 7) sts.
With RS facing, rejoin yarn to rem sts, bind off
center 23 (25: 25: 27: 27) sts, patt to end.
Complete to match first side, reversing shapings.

LEFT FRONT
Lower section
Cast on 48 (51: 54: 57: 60) sts using size 2 (3mm)
needles.
Row 1 (RS): P0 (0: 1: 0: 0), K1 (0: 2: 2: 1), [P2, K2]
2 (3: 3: 4: 5) times, [P4, K3] twice, P2, [K3, P4]
twice, K3, P2, K3, P1.
Row 2: K1, P3, K2, [P3, K4] twice, P3, K2, [P3, K4]
twice, [P2, K2] 2 (3: 3: 4: 5) times, P1 (0: 2: 2: 1),
K0 (0: 1: 0: 0).
These 2 rows form rib.
Work in rib for a further 8 rows, ending with a WS
row.
Change to size 3 (3.25mm) needles.
Work in rib for a further 10 rows, ending with a
WS row.
Row 21 (RS): Rib 11 (14: 17: 20: 23), P2tog, K3,
P2tog, rib 12, P2tog, K3, P2tog, rib to end.
44 (47: 50: 53: 56) sts.
Keeping rib correct as set, work 19 rows, ending
with a WS row.
Row 41 (RS): Rib 10 (13: 16: 19: 22), P2tog, K3,
P2tog, rib 10, P2tog, K3, P2tog, rib to end.
40 (43: 46: 49: 52) sts.
Keeping rib correct as set, work 15 rows, ending
with a WS row.
Bind off knitwise.
Upper section
With **WS** facing (so that ridge is formed on RS of
work) and using size 3 (3.25mm) needles, pick up
and knit 40 (43: 46: 49: 52) sts across bound-off
edge of lower section.
Beg with a K row, work in St st for 4 rows, dec 1 st
at end of 3rd of these rows and ending with a WS

Special tip

PICKING UP AND KNITTING STITCHES

The neat seams above the ribbed welts of this cardigan are created by binding off the ribbed stitches and then picking up the stitches again, ready to knit the upper sections. However, to create the ridged seam, these stitches have been picked up with the **wrong** side of the work facing. This means the bound-off edge will sit proud of the knitting on the right side of the work forming a ridge.

Whether you are picking up stitches with the right or wrong side facing, it is important to pick them up neatly and evenly. When picking up stitches across a bound-off edge, as here, pick up one stitch for every bound-off stitch, inserting the right needle point through the center of each bound-off stitch. When picking up stitches along a row-end edge, as for the front band of this cardigan, make sure you insert the needle into the knitting the same amount inside the edge for every stitch. Ideally, you should pick up the stitches by inserting the right needle point between the first and second stitches but, when working with very thick yarns, it is sometimes better to insert the needle point through the center of the edge stitch instead.

row. *39 (42: 45: 48: 51) sts.*
Patt as foll:
Row 1 (RS): K3 (0: 3: 0: 3), *K2tog, yo, K4, rep from * to end.
Beg with a P row, work in St st for 7 rows, inc 1 st at beg of 2nd of these rows **and at same time** dec 1 st at end of 6th (4th: 6th: 4th: 4th) of these rows. *39 (42: 45: 48: 51) sts.*
Row 9 (RS): Inc in first st, K0 (3: 0: 3: 0), *K2tog, yo, K4, rep from * to last 2 sts, K2.
40 (43: 46: 49: 52) sts.
Beg with a P row, work in St st for 7 rows, inc 1 st at beg of 6th of these rows **and at same time** dec 1 st at end of 6th (2nd: 6th: 2nd: 2nd) of these rows. *40 (43: 46: 49: 52) sts.*
Last 16 rows form patt and start side seam and front slope shaping.
Cont in patt, shaping side seams by inc 1 st at beg of 5th and 4 foll 6th rows **and at same time** dec 1 st at end of 7th (3rd: 7th: next: 3rd) and every foll 8th row, taking inc sts into patt.
42 (44: 48: 50: 53) sts.
Work 13 (15: 15: 17: 17) rows, dec 1 st at end of 2nd (6th: 2nd: 4th: 6th) and foll 8th row, ending with a WS row. *40 (42: 46: 48: 51) sts.* (Left front should match back to beg of armhole shaping.)
Shape armhole
Keeping patt correct, bind off 3 (4: 4: 5: 5) sts at beg of next row. *37 (38: 42: 43: 46) sts.*
Work 1 row.
Dec 1 st at armhole edge of next 5 (5: 7: 7: 9) rows, then on foll 4 (5: 5: 6: 6) alt rows **and at same time** dec 1 st at front slope edge of 3rd (5th: next: next: 3rd) and every foll 8th row.
26 (26: 27: 27: 28) sts.
Dec 1 st at front slope edge **only** of 6th (6th: 8th: 6th: 6th) and every foll 8th row until 21 (21: 22: 22: 23) sts rem.
Cont even until left front matches back to start of shoulder shaping, ending with a WS row.

Shape shoulder
Bind off 7 (7: 7: 7: 8) sts at beg of next and foll alt row.
Work 1 row.
Bind off rem 7 (7: 8: 8: 7) sts.

RIGHT FRONT
Lower section
Cast on 48 (51: 54: 57: 60) sts using size 2 (3mm) needles.
Row 1 (RS): P1, K3, P2, [K3, P4] twice, K3, P2, [K3, P4] twice, [K2, P2] 2 (3: 3: 4: 5) times, K1 (0: 2: 2: 1), P0 (0: 1: 0: 0).
Row 2: K0 (0: 1: 0: 0), P1 (0: 2: 2: 1), [K2, P2] 2 (3: 3: 4: 5) times, [K4, P3] twice, K2, [P3, K4] twice, P3, K2, P3, K1.
These 2 rows form rib.
Work in rib for a further 8 rows, ending with a WS row.
Change to size 3 (3.25mm) needles.
Work in rib for a further 10 rows, ending with a WS row.
Row 21 (RS): Rib 11, P2tog, K3, P2tog, rib 12, P2tog, K3, P2tog, rib to end. *44 (47: 50: 53: 56) sts.*
Keeping rib correct as set, work 19 rows, ending with a WS row.
Row 41 (RS): [Rib 10, P2tog, K3, P2tog] twice, rib to end. *40 (43: 46: 49: 52) sts.*
Keeping rib correct as set, work 15 rows, ending with a WS row.
Bind off knitwise.
Upper section
With **WS** facing (so that ridge is formed on RS of work) and using size 3 (3.25mm) needles, pick up and knit 40 (43: 46: 49: 52) sts across bound-off edge of lower section.
Beg with a K row, work in St st for 4 rows, dec 1 st at beg of 3rd of these rows and ending with a WS row. *39 (42: 45: 48: 51) sts.*
Patt as foll:

Row 1 (RS): K3, *K2tog, yo, K4, rep from * to last 6 (3: 6: 3: 6) sts, K2tog, yo, K4 (1: 4: 1: 4).
Beg with a P row, work in St st for 7 rows, inc 1 st at end of 2nd of these rows **and at same time** dec 1 st at beg of 6th (4th: 6th: 4th: 4th) of these rows. *39 (42: 45: 48: 51) sts.*
Row 9 (RS): K5, *K2tog, yo, K4, rep from * to last 4 (7: 4: 7: 4) sts, K2tog, yo, K1 (4: 1: 4: 1), inc in last st. *40 (43: 46: 49: 52) sts.*
Beg with a P row, work in St st for 7 rows, inc 1 st at end of 6th of these rows **and at same time** dec 1 st at beg of 6th (2nd: 6th: 2nd: 2nd) of these rows. *40 (43: 46: 49: 52) sts.*
Last 16 rows form patt and start side seam and front slope shaping.
Complete to match left front, reversing shapings.

SLEEVES (both alike)
Lower section
Cast on 54 (54: 56: 58: 58) sts using size 2 (3mm) needles.
Row 1 (RS): K1 (1: 2: 3: 3), *P2, K3, rep from * to last 3 (3: 4: 5: 5) sts, P2, K1 (1: 2: 3: 3).
Row 2: P1 (1: 2: 3: 3), *K2, P3, rep from * to last 3 (3: 4: 5: 5) sts, K2, P1 (1: 2: 3: 3).
These 2 rows form rib.
Work in rib for a further 8 rows, ending with a WS row.
Change to size 3 (3.25mm) needles.
Work in rib, shaping sides by inc 1 st at each end of 5th (3rd: 3rd: 3rd: 3rd) and every foll 14th (12th: 12th: 12th: 12th) row until there are 58 (60: 62: 64: 64) sts, taking inc sts into rib.
Work a further 9 (1: 1: 1: 1) rows, ending with a WS row.
Bind off knitwise.

Upper section

With **WS** facing (so that ridge is formed on RS of work) and using size 3 (3.25mm) needles, pick up and knit 59 (61: 63: 65: 65) sts across bound-off edge of lower section.

Beg with a K row, work in St st for 6 rows, inc 1 (0: 0: 0: 0) st at each end of 3rd of these rows and ending with a WS row. *61 (61: 63: 65: 65) sts.*

Patt as foll:

Row 1 (RS): K5 (5: 0: 1: 1), *K2tog, yo, K4, rep from * to last 8 (8: 3: 4: 4) sts, K2tog, yo, K6 (6: 1: 2: 2).

Beg with a P row, work in St st for 7 rows, inc 0 (1: 1: 1: 1) st at each end of 4th of these rows and ending with a WS row. *61 (63: 65: 67: 67) sts.*

Row 9 (RS): K2 (3: 4: 5: 5), *K2tog, yo, K4, rep from * to last 5 (6: 7: 8: 8) sts, K2tog, yo, K3 (4: 5: 6: 6).

Beg with a P row, work in St st for 7 rows, inc 1 (0: 0: 0: 0) st at each end of 2nd of these rows and ending with a WS row. *63 (63: 65: 67: 67) sts.*

Last 16 rows form patt and start sleeve shaping.

Cont in patt, shaping sides by inc 1 st at each end of 7th (next: next: next: next) and every foll 12th row to 75 (73: 79: 81: 71) sts, then on every foll - (10th: -: -: 10th) row until there are - (77: -: -: 83) sts, taking inc sts into patt.

Cont even until sleeve measures 17³/₄ (17³/₄: 18: 18: 18)in/45 (45: 46: 46: 46)cm **from cast-on edge of lower section**, ending with a WS row.

Shape top

Keeping patt correct, bind off 3 (4: 4: 5: 5) sts at beg of next 2 rows. *69 (69: 71: 71: 73) sts.*

Dec 1 st at each end of next 3 rows, then on foll alt row, then on every foll 4th row until 47 (47: 49: 49: 51) sts rem.

Work 1 row, ending with a WS row.

Dec 1 st at each end of next and every foll alt row to 43 sts, then on foll 5 rows, ending with a WS row.

Bind off rem 33 sts.

FINISHING

PRESS as described on the information page 138.

Join both shoulder seams using back stitch, or mattress stitch if preferred.

Front band

With RS facing and using size 2 (3mm) circular needle, starting and ending at cast-on edges, pick up and knit 42 sts up right front opening edge to top of lower section, 98 (100: 102: 104: 106) sts up right front slope to shoulder, 31 (33: 33: 35: 35) sts from back, 98 (100: 102: 104: 106) sts down left front slope to top of lower section, then 42 sts down left front opening edge.

311 (317: 321: 327: 331) sts.

Beg with a P row, work in St st for 6 rows.

Bind off.
See information page 138 for finishing
instructions, setting in sleeves using the set-
in method. Cut ribbon into 2 equal lengths and
attach one end of each piece to inside of front
opening edge level with top of lower section.

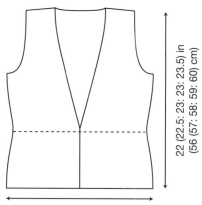

22 (22.5: 23: 23: 23.5) in
(56 (57: 58: 59: 60) cm)

16.5 (17.5: 18.5: 19.5: 20.5) in
(42 (45: 47.5: 50: 52.5) cm)

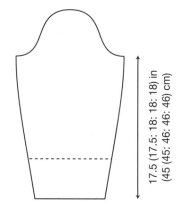

17.5 (17.5: 18: 18: 18) in
(45 (45: 46: 46: 46) cm)

Elfin

A very feminine pair of patterns, the cardigan is knitted in a tweed yarn with a frilled edge and cuffs in *Kidsilk Haze*. The cardigan is held together with hooks and eyes, hidden under the ruffle. The sweater is knitted entirely in the mohair/silk yarn, used double, with a multi-frilled ruffle, knitted with the yarn single, at the cuffs and around the polo neck. Knitters will enjoy the fun of working the frills.

YARN AND SIZES

	XS	S	M	L	XL	
To fit bust	32	34	36	38	40	in
	81	86	91	97	102	cm

Sweater
Light-weight (CYCA Fine) yarn
Rowan *Kidsilk Haze** (70% super kid mohair, 30% silk; 229yd/25g) in Majestic 589

	9	10	10	11	12	balls

*Yarn is used double EXCEPT where stated

Cardigan
DK (CYCA Light) yarn and Lightweight (CYCA Fine) yarn
Rowan *Felted Tweed* (50% merino wool, 25% alpaca wool, 25% viscose; 191yd/50g) and *Kidsilk Haze* (70% super kid mohair, 30% silk; 229yd/25g)

A Felted Carbon 159	6	6	6	7	7	balls
B **KSH Anthracite 639	2	2	3	3	3	balls

**Use *Kidsilk Haze* SINGLE throughout (Originally photographed in Rowan *Felted Tweed* Dragon 147 and Rowan *Kidsilk Haze* Drab 588)

NEEDLES
1 pair size 3 (3.25mm) needles
1 pair size 5 (3.75mm) needles

EXTRAS
Cardigan only: 10 hook-and-eye fasteners

GAUGE
23 sts and 32 rows to 4in/10cm measured over stockinette stitch using size 5 (3.75mm) needles *or size necessary to obtain correct gauge.*

Sweater

BACK

Cast on 105 (111: 117: 123: 129) sts using size 3 (3.25mm) needles and yarn DOUBLE.

Row 1 (RS): K1, *P1, K2, rep from * to last 2 sts, P1, K1.

Row 2: P1, *K1, P2, rep from * to last 2 sts, K1, P1.

Rep last 2 rows 6 times more, ending with a WS row.

Change to size 5 (3.75mm) needles.

Beg with a K row, work in St st for 8 rows, ending with a WS row.

Place markers on 26th (28th: 30th: 32nd: 34th) sts in from each end of last row.

Next row (RS): K2, K2tog, [K to within 1 st of marked st, sl 2 as though to K2tog, K1, p2sso] twice, K to last 4 sts, K2tog tbl, K2.

Work 11 rows.

Rep last 12 rows once more, then first of these rows (the dec row) again. *87 (93: 99: 105: 111) sts.*

Work 13 rows, ending with a WS row.

Next row (RS): K2, M1, [K to marked st, M1, K marked st, M1] twice, K to last 2 sts, M1, K2.

Work 15 rows.

Rep last 16 rows once more, then first of these rows (the inc row) again.

105 (111: 117: 123: 129) sts.

Cont even until back measures 13³/₄ (14: 14: 14¹/₂: 14¹/₂)in/35 (36: 36: 37: 37)cm, ending with a WS row.

Shape armholes

Bind off 4 (5: 5: 6: 6) sts at beg of next 2 rows. *97 (101: 107: 111: 117) sts.*

Dec 1 st at each end of next 5 (5: 7: 7: 9) rows, then on foll 4 (5: 5: 6: 6) alt rows.

79 (81: 83: 85: 87) sts.

Cont even until armhole measures 8 (8: 8¹/₄: 8¹/₄: 8³/₄)in/20 (20: 21: 21: 22)cm, ending with a WS row.

Shape shoulders and back neck

Bind off 6 (6: 6: 6: 7) sts at beg of next 2 rows. *67 (69: 71: 73: 73) sts.*

Next row (RS): Bind off 6 (6: 6: 6: 7) sts, K until there are 10 (10: 11: 11: 10) sts on right needle and turn, leaving rem sts on a holder.

Work each side of neck separately.

Bind off 4 sts at beg of next row.

Bind off rem 6 (6: 7: 7: 6) sts.

With RS facing, rejoin yarn to rem sts, bind off center 35 (37: 37: 39: 39) sts, K to end.

Complete to match first side, reversing shapings.

FRONT

Work as given for back until 16 (16: 16: 18: 18) rows less have been worked than on back to start of shoulder shaping, ending with a WS row.

Shape neck

Next row (RS): K28 (28: 29: 30: 31) and turn, leaving rem sts on a holder.

Work each side of neck separately.

Dec 1 st at neck edge of next 8 rows, then on foll 2 (2: 2: 3: 3) alt rows. *18 (18: 19: 19: 20) sts.*

Work 3 rows, ending with a WS row.

Shape shoulder

Bind off 6 (6: 6: 6: 7) sts at beg of next and foll alt row.

Work 1 row. Bind off rem 6 (6: 7: 7: 6) sts.

With RS facing, rejoin yarn to rem sts, bind off center 23 (25: 25: 25: 25) sts, K to end.

Complete to match first side, reversing shapings.

SLEEVES (both alike)
Frill

Cast on 225 (225: 233: 241: 241) sts **loosely** using size 5 (3.75mm) needles and yarn SINGLE.

****Beg with a K row, work in St st for 3 rows.

Row 4 (WS): P1, [P2tog] to end.

Work 3 rows.

Row 8: As row 4. *57 (57: 59: 61: 61) sts.*

Break yarn and leave sts on a holder.

Make a further 2 frills in same way.****

Main section

Using size 3 (3.25mm) needles and yarn DOUBLE, K across 57 (57: 59: 61: 61) sts of first frill.

******Beg with a P row, work in St st for 3 rows.

***Holding WS of next frill against RS of work, K to end, working each st of next frill tog with corresponding st on left needle.

Work 3 rows.

Rep from *** once more.

Change to size 5 (3.75mm) needles.

Work a further 8 rows.

Next row (inc) (RS): K2, M1, K to last 2 sts, M1, K2.

Working all increases as set by last row, cont in St st, shaping sides by inc 1 st at each end of every foll 10th (10th: 10th: 10th: 8th) row to 67 (79: 79: 81: 71) sts, then on every foll 12th (-: 12th: 12th:

10th) row until there are 77 (-: 81: 83: 85) sts.

Cont even until sleeve measures 16 (16: 16½: 16½: 16½)in/41 (41: 42: 42: 42)cm from top of third frill, ending with a WS row.

Shape top

Bind off 4 (5: 5: 6: 6) sts at beg of next 2 rows. *69 (69: 71: 71: 73) sts.*

Dec 1 st at each end of next 3 rows, then on foll 3 alt rows, then on every foll 4th row until 45 (45: 47: 47: 49) sts rem.

Work 1 row, ending with a WS row.

Dec 1 st at each end of next and every foll alt row to 39 sts, then on foll 3 rows, ending with a WS row.

Bind off rem 33 sts.

FINISHING

PRESS as described on the information page 138.

Join both shoulder seams using back stitch, or mattress stitch if preferred.

Collar
Frill

Cast on 425 (433: 433: 465: 465) sts **loosely** using size 5 (3.75mm) needles and yarn SINGLE.

Work as given for sleeve frills from ** to **, noting that there are 107 (109: 109: 117: 117) sts rem for each frill.

Main section

Using size 5 (3.75mm) needles and yarn DOUBLE, K across 107 (109: 109: 117: 117) sts of first frill.

****Beg with a P row, work in St st for 3 rows.

*****Holding WS of next frill against RS of work, K to end, working each st of next frill tog with corresponding st on left needle.

Work 3 rows.

Rep from ***** once more.

Cont in St st until collar measures 5in/12cm from top of third frill.

Change to size 3 (3.25mm) needles.

Cont in St st until collar measures 8¾in/22cm

from top of third frill. Bind off.

Join row end edges of collar. Matching collar seam to center back neck, sew bound-off edge of collar to neck edge.

See information page 138 for finishing instructions, setting in sleeves using the set-in method.

Cardigan

BACK

Cast on 105 (111: 117: 123: 129) sts using size 3 (3.25mm) needles and yarn A.

Work as given for back of sweater to start of shoulder shaping, ending with a WS row.

Shape shoulders and back neck

Bind off 8 sts at beg of next 2 rows.

63 (65: 67: 69: 71) sts.

Next row (RS): Bind off 8 sts, K until there are 11 (11: 12: 12: 13) sts on right needle and turn, leaving rem sts on a holder.

Work each side of neck separately.

Bind off 4 sts at beg of next row.

Bind off rem 7 (7: 8: 8: 9) sts.

With RS facing, rejoin yarn to rem sts, bind off center 25 (27: 27: 29: 29) sts, K to end.

Complete to match first side, reversing shapings.

LEFT FRONT

Cast on 53 (56: 59: 62: 65) sts using size 3 (3.25mm) needles and yarn A.

Row 1 (RS): K1, *P1, K2, rep from * to last st, P1.

Row 2: K1, *P2, K1, rep from * to last st, P1.

Rep last 2 rows 6 times more, ending with a WS row.

Change to size 5 (3.75mm) needles.

Beg with a K row, work in St st for 8 rows, ending with a WS row.

Place marker on 26th (28th: 30th: 32nd: 34th) st in from end (side seam edge) of last row.

Next row (RS): K2, K2tog, K to within 1 st of marked st, sl 2 as though to K2tog, K1, p2sso, K to end.

Work 11 rows.

Rep last 12 rows once more, then first of these rows (the dec row) again. *44 (47: 50: 53: 56) sts.*

Work 13 rows, ending with a WS row.

Next row (RS): K2, M1, K to marked st, M1, K marked st, M1, K to end.

Work 15 rows.

Rep last 16 rows once more, then first of these rows (the inc row) again. *53 (56: 59: 62: 65) sts.*

Cont even until 12 rows fewer have been worked than on back to beg of armhole shaping, ending with a WS row.

Shape front slope

Next row (RS): K to last 4 sts, K2tog tbl, K2.

Working all front slope decreases as set by last row, dec 1 st at end of 4th and foll 4th row. *50 (53: 56: 59: 62) sts.*

Work 3 rows, ending with a WS row.

Shape armhole

Bind off 4 (5: 5: 6: 6) sts at beg and dec 1 st at end of next row. *45 (47: 50: 52: 55) sts.*

Work 1 row.

Dec 1 st at armhole edge of next 5 (5: 7: 7: 9) rows, then on foll 4 (5: 5: 6: 6) alt rows **and at same time** dec 1 st at front slope edge of 3rd and every foll 4th row. *33 (33: 34: 34: 35) sts.*

Dec 1 st at front slope edge only on 2nd (4th: 2nd: 4th: 2nd) and every foll 4th row until 23 (23: 24: 24: 25) sts rem.

Cont even until left front matches back to start of shoulder shaping, ending with a WS row.

Shape shoulder

Bind off 8 sts at beg of next and foll alt row.

Work 1 row.

Bind off rem 7 (7: 8: 8: 9) sts.

RIGHT FRONT

Cast on 53 (56: 59: 62: 65) sts using size 3

(3.25mm) needles and yarn A.

Row 1 (RS): P1, *K2, P1, rep from * to last st, K1.
Row 2: P1, *K1, P2, rep from * to last st, K1.

Rep last 2 rows 6 times more, ending with a WS row.

Change to size 5 (3.75mm) needles.

Beg with a K row, work in St st for 8 rows, ending with a WS row.

Place marker on 26th (28th: 30th: 32nd: 34th) sts in from beg (side seam edge) of last row.

Next row (RS): K to within 1 st of marked st, sl 2 as though to K2tog, K1, p2sso, K to last 4 sts, K2tog tbl, K2.

Complete to match left front, reversing shapings.

SLEEVES (both alike)
Frill
Cast on 225 (225: 233: 241: 241) sts **loosely** using size 5 (3.75mm) needles and yarn B SINGLE.

Work as given for frills of sweater sleeves from ** to **.

Main section
Using size 5 (3.75mm) needles and yarn A, K across 57 (57: 59: 61: 61) sts of first frill.

Complete as given for sleeves of sweater from ******.

FINISHING
PRESS as described on the information page 138.

Join both shoulder seams using back stitch, or mattress stitch if preferred.

Right front band
First frill
Cast on 293 (297: 305: 309: 317) sts **loosely** using size 5 (3.75mm) needles and yarn B SINGLE.

**Beg with a K row, work in St st for 3 rows.
Row 4 (WS): P1, [P2tog] to end.

Work 3 rows.

Row 8: As row 4.** *74 (75: 77: 78: 80)* sts.

Break yarn and leave sts on a holder.

Special tip

MAKING FRILLS

When knitting the frills of this design, it may seem daunting to cast on so many stitches. But, to make the frill, these stitches will soon be decreased down to a much more manageable number. To ensure that the edge of the frill is full and does not pull in, take great care to cast on very loosely—especially in a yarn such as *Kidsilk Haze*. You may prefer to cast on using needles one or two sizes larger than stated just to make sure the edge is not too tight. And, if there seem too many stitches to fit easily onto straight needles, work the first few rows of the frills on a circular needle, changing to straight needles once the number of stitches has been decreased.

Second frill

Cast on 253 (257: 265: 269: 277) sts **loosely** using size 5 (3.75mm) needles and yarn B SINGLE.
Work as given for first frill from ** to **.
64 (65: 67: 68: 70) sts.
Break yarn and leave sts on a holder.

Third frill

Cast on 597 (609: 617: 629: 637) sts **loosely** using size 5 (3.75mm) needles and yarn B SINGLE.
Work as given for first frill from ** to **.
150 (153: 155: 158: 160) sts.
Break off yarn B and join in yarn A.
Beg with a K row, work in St st for 2 rows.
Next row (RS): K77 (78: 80: 81: 83), wrap next st (by slipping next st from left needle to right needle, taking yarn to opposite side of work between needles and then slipping same st back onto left needle) and turn.
Next row: Purl.
Next row: Holding WS of first frill against RS of work, K tog each st of first frill tog with corresponding st on left needle until all 74 (75: 77: 78: 80) sts of frill have been attached, wrap next st and turn.
Next row: Purl.
Next row: K71 (72: 74: 75: 77), wrap next st and turn.
Next row: Purl.
Next row: Holding WS of second frill against RS of work, K tog each st of second frill tog with corresponding st on left needle until all 64 (65: 67: 68: 70) sts of frill have been attached, K4, wrap next st and turn.
Next row: Purl.
Work in St st for 2 rows across all sts.
Bind off.

Left front band

Work as for right front band, reversing shaping.
Join longer row end edges of bands, and frill seams. Matching band seam to center back neck,

sew bound-off edge of bands to front opening and
back neck edges.

See information page 138 for finishing
instructions, setting in sleeves using the set-in
method.

Attach hook-and-eye fasteners to close front
opening edges, positioning top fastener level with
start of front slope shaping, lowest fasteners just
above cast-on edge, and rem 8 fasteners evenly
spaced between.

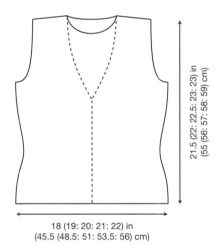

21.5 (22: 22.5: 23: 23) in
(55 (56: 57: 58: 59) cm)

18 (19: 20: 21: 22) in
(45.5 (48.5: 51: 53.5: 56) cm)

17.5 (17.5: 18: 18: 18) in
(45 (45: 46: 46: 46) cm)

Erin

Cable patterns are perennially popular as there is something very satisfying about working the twists of the cable. They look more complicated to knit than they are, particularly when, as here, you have only a few really large ones. This classic polo neck sweater in *All Seasons Cotton* has large 10-stitch cables for the adult sizes and 8-stitch cables for the children's sizes.

YARN AND SIZES

To fit age 9–10 10–11 12–13 13–14 years

	XS	S	M	L	XL	
To fit bust	32	34	36	38	40	in
	81	86	91	97	102	cm

Worsted (CYCA Medium) yarn
Rowan *All Seasons Cotton* **(60% cotton, 40% acrylic/microfiber; 98yd/50g)**
Children's in Strawberry 248

8	9	9	10	balls

(Originally photographed in Sizzling 179)

Ladies' in Bleached 182

12	12	13	13	14	balls

(Originally photographed in Organic 178)

NEEDLES

1 pair size 7 (4.5mm) needles
1 pair size 8 (5mm) needles
Size 7 (4.5mm) circular needle
Cable needle

GAUGE

17 sts and 24 rows to 4in/10cm measured over stockinette stitch using size 8 (5mm) needles *or size necessary to obtain correct gauge.*

Pattern note: The pattern is written for the 4 children's sizes, followed by the ladies' sizes in **bold**. Where only one figure appears this applies to all sizes in that group.

SPECIAL ABBREVIATIONS

C8B = Cable 8 back Slip next 4 sts onto cable needle and leave at back of work, K4, then K4 from cable needle.
C10B = Cable 10 back Slip next 5 sts onto cable needle and leave at back of work, K5, then K5 from cable needle.

BACK

Cast on 78 (82: 86: 90: **94: 98: 102: 106: 110**) sts using size 7 (4.5mm) needles.

Row 1 (RS): K0 (**0: 0: 0: 6: 8**), P2 (4: 6: 8: **3: 5: 7: 3: 3**), *K8 (**10**), P3, rep from * to last 10 (1: 3: 5: **0: 2: 4: 6: 8**) sts, K8 (0: 0: 0: **0: 0: 0: 6: 8**), P2 (1: 3: 5: **0: 2: 4: 0: 0**).

Row 2: P0 (**0: 0: 0: 6: 8**), K2 (4: 6: 8: **3: 5: 7: 3: 3**), *P8 (**10**), K3, rep from * to last 10 (1: 3: 5: **0: 2: 4: 6: 8**) sts, P8 (0: 0: 0: **0: 0: 0: 6: 8**), K2 (1: 3: 5: **0: 2: 4: 0: 0**).

These 2 rows form rib.

Work in rib for a further 12 (**14**) rows, dec 1 st at each end of 5th (5th: 7th: 7th: **7th: 7th: 7th: 9th: 9th**) of these rows.

Change to size 8 (5mm) needles.

Cont in rib as set for a further 10 (**14**) rows **and at same time** dec 1 st at each end of next (next: 3rd: 3rd: **next: next: next: 3rd: 3rd**) and foll 8th (8th: 0: 0: **8th**) row. 72 (76: 82: 86: **88: 92: 96: 100: 104**) sts and 24 (**30**) rows of rib completed.

Children's sizes only

Next row (RS): [K2tog] 0 (0: 1: 1) time, rib 10 (12: 13: 15), [C8B, rib 14] twice, C8B, rib 10 (12: 13: 15), [K2tog] 0 (0: 1: 1) time. *72 (76: 80: 84) sts.*

Ladies' sizes only

Next row (RS): Rib (13: 15: 17: 19: 21), [C10B, rib 16] twice, C10B, rib (13: 15: 17: 19: 21).

All sizes

Last row sets position of cables.

Working cables as set by last row on every foll 18th (**20th**) row, cont in rib with cables as foll:

Dec 1 st at each end of 6th (6th: 8th: 8th: **2nd: 2nd: 2nd: 4th: 4th**) row.

*70 (74: 78: 82: **86: 90: 94: 98: 102**) sts.*

Work 7 (9: 9: 9: **13**) rows, ending with a WS row.

Inc 1 st at each end of next and every foll 8th row until there are 78 (82: 86: 90: **94: 98: 102: 106: 110**) sts, taking inc sts into rib.

Cont even until back measures 12 (12$\frac{1}{4}$: 12$\frac{1}{2}$: 13: **13$\frac{1}{2}$: 13$\frac{3}{4}$: 13$\frac{3}{4}$: 14: 14**)in/30 (31: 32: 33: **34: 35:**

35: 36: 36)cm, ending with a WS row.

Shape armholes

Keeping patt correct, bind off 2 (2: 3: 3: **3: 4: 4: 4: 5**) sts at beg of next 2 rows.

*74 (78: 80: 84: **88: 90: 94: 98: 100**) sts.*

Dec 1 st at each end of next 3 (**5**) rows, then on foll 1 (2: 2: 3: **2: 2: 3: 4: 4**) alt rows.

*66 (68: 70: 72: **74: 76: 78: 80: 82**) sts.*

Cont even until armhole measures 6³/₄ (7: 7¹/₂: 8: **8¹/₄: 8¹/₄: 8³/₄: 8³/₄: 9**)in/17 (18: 19: 20: **21: 21: 22: 22: 23**)cm, ending with a WS row.

Shape shoulders and back neck

Bind off 6 (6: 6: 7: **7**) sts at beg of next 2 rows.

*54 (56: 58: 58: **60: 62: 64: 66: 68**) sts.*

Next row (RS): Bind off 6 (6: 6: 7: **7**) sts, patt until there are 10 (11: 11: 10: **10: 10: 11: 11: 12**) sts on right needle and turn, leaving rem sts on a holder.

Work each side of neck separately.

Bind off 4 sts at beg of next row.

Bind off rem 6 (7: 7: 6: **6: 6: 7: 7: 8**) sts.

With RS facing, rejoin yarn to rem sts, bind off center 22 (22: 24: 24: **26: 28: 28: 30: 30**) sts working [K2tog] 4 (**5**) times across top of central cable, patt to end.

Work to match first side, reversing shapings.

FRONT

Work as given for back until 12 (**14: 14: 14: 16: 16**) rows less have been worked than on back to start of shoulder shaping, ending with a WS row.

Shape neck

Next row (RS): Patt 23 (24: 24: 25: **26: 26: 27: 28: 29**) sts and turn, leaving rem sts on a holder.

Work each side of neck separately.

Dec 1 st at neck edge of next 4 rows, then on foll 1 (**2: 2: 2: 3: 3**) alt rows.

*18 (19: 19: 20: **20: 20: 21: 21: 22**) sts.*

Work 5 rows, ending with a WS row.

Shape shoulder

Bind off 6 (6: 6: 7: **7**) sts at beg of next and foll alt row.

Work 1 row.

Bind off rem 6 (7: 7: 6: **6: 6: 7: 7: 8**) sts.

With RS facing, rejoin yarn to rem sts, bind off center 20 (20: 22: 22: **22: 24: 24: 24: 24**) sts working [K2tog] 4 (**5**) times across top of central cable, patt to end.

Work to match first side, reversing shapings.

SLEEVES (both alike)

Cast on 40 (40: 42: 42: **50: 50: 52: 54: 54**) sts using size 7 (4.5mm) needles.

Row 1 (RS): K0 (1: 1: 2: 3: **3**), P0 (0: 1: 1: **3**), [K5, P3] twice, K8 (**10**), [P3, K5] twice, P0 (0: 1: 1: **3**), K0 (1: 1: 2: 3: **3**).

Row 2: P0 (1: 1: 2: 3: **3**), K0 (0: 1: 1: **3**), [P5, K3] twice, P8 (**10**), [K3, P5] twice, K0 (0: 1: 1: **3**), P0 (1: **1: 2: 3: 3**).

These 2 rows form rib.

Work in rib for a further 4 rows.

Change to size 8 (5mm) needles.

Work a further 14 (**18**) rows, inc 1 st at each end of 11th of these rows.

*42 (42: 44: 44: **52: 52: 54: 56: 56**) sts.*

Next row (RS): P17 (17: 18: 18: **21: 21: 22: 23: 23**), K8 (**10**), P17 (17: 18: 18: **21: 21: 22: 23: 23**).

Next row: K17 (17: 18: 18: **21: 21: 22: 23: 23**), P8 (**10**), K17 (17: 18: 18: **21: 21: 22: 23: 23**).

These 2 rows set position of central cable and rev St st.

Work a further 4 rows as set.

Next row (RS): [Inc in first st] 0 (**1**) times, P17 (17: 18: 18: **20: 20: 21: 22: 22**), [C8B] 1 (**0**) times, [C10B] 0 (**1**) times, P17 (17: 18: 18: **20: 20: 21: 22: 22**), [inc in last st] 0 (**1**) times.

*42 (42: 44: 44: **54: 54: 56: 58: 58**) sts.*

Last row sets cable.

Working cables as set by last row on every foll 18th (**20th**) row, cont in rev St st with cable as foll:

Inc 1 st at each end of 4th (2nd: 4th: 2nd: **14th: 12th: 12th: 12th: 12th**) and every foll 14th (12th: 14th: 12th: **14th: 12th: 12th: 12th: 10th**) row to

50 (52: 50: 52: **60: 62: 68: 70: 72**) sts, then on every foll - (-: 12th: 10th: **12th: 10th: -: -: -**) row until there are - (-: 54: 56: **64: 66: -: -: -**) sts.
Cont even until sleeve measures 14 (14½: 15½: 15¾: **17¾: 17¾: 18: 18: 18**)in/35 (37: 39: 40: **45: 45: 46: 46: 46**)cm, ending with a WS row.

Shape top

Keeping patt correct, bind off 2 (2: 3: 3: **3: 4: 4: 4: 5**) sts at beg of next 2 rows.
46 (48: 48: 50: 58: 58: 60: 62: 62) sts.

Dec 1 st at each end of next 3 rows, then on foll 2 alt rows, then on every foll 4th row until 32 (34: 32: 34: **40: 40: 42: 46: 44**) sts rem.
Work 1 row, ending with a WS row.
Dec 1 st at each end of next and foll 1 (2: 1: 2: **1: 1: 2: 4: 3**) alt rows, then on foll 3 rows. *22 (30) sts.*
Bind off 3 (**4**) sts at beg of next 2 rows.
Bind off rem 16 (**22**) sts.

FINISHING

PRESS all pieces as described on the information page 138.
Join both shoulder seams using back stitch, or mattress stitch if preferred.

Neckband

With RS facing and size 7 (4.5mm) circular needle, starting at left shoulder seam, pick up and knit 10 (10: 14: 14: **15: 13: 13: 18: 18**) sts down left side of neck, 16 (16: 18: 18: **17: 19: 19: 19: 19**) sts from front, 10 (10: 14: 14: **15: 13: 13: 18: 18**) sts up right side of neck, then 26 (26: 28: 28: **29: 31: 31: 33: 33**) sts from back.
62 (62: 74: 74: 76: 76: 76: 88: 88) sts.

Round 1 (RS): K1 (1: 0: 0: **0**), P3 (**3: 2: 2: 1: 1**), [K3, P3] 2 (2: 3: 3: **3: 3: 3: 4: 4**) times, K4 (**5**), [P3, K3] 4 (4: 5: 5: **5: 5: 5: 6: 6**) times, P3, K4 (**5**), [P3, K3] 1 (1: 2: 2: **2**) times, P3 (3: 0: 0: **0: 1: 1: 2: 2**), K2 (2: 0: 0: **0**).
Rep this round for 4 (**5**)in/10 (**12**)cm.
Bind off.

See information page 138 for finishing instructions, setting in sleeves using the set-in method.

15.5 (16: 17: 18: **18.5: 19.5: 20: 21: 22**) in (39 (41: 43.5: 46: **46.5: 49: 51: 53.5: 56**) cm)

18.5 (19.5: 20: 21: **21.5: 22: 22.5: 23: 23**) in (47 (49: 51: 53: **55: 56: 57: 58: 59**) cm)

14 (14.5: 15: 15.5: **17.5: 17.5: 18: 18: 18**) in (35 (37: 39: 40: **45: 45: 46: 46: 46**) cm)

Maggie

This little cropped top with its split neck fastened with a narrow silk ribbon, is knitted in soft and luxurious *Kidsilk Haze* used double. Knitted in stockinette stitch, with a short, broad ribbed welt, it is a figure hugging design. It is ideal for wearing with a flared skirt or cropped pants.

YARN AND SIZES

To fit bust	XS	S	M	L	XL	
	32	34	36	38	40	in
	81	86	91	97	102	cm

Lightweight (CYCA Fine) yarn
Rowan *Kidsilk Haze* (70% super kid mohair, 30% silk; 229yd/25g) in Mist 636

4	5	5	5	6	balls

(Originally photographed in Tropic 602)

NEEDLES

1 pair size 3 (3mm) needles
1 pair size 5 (3.75mm) needles

EXTRAS

23¾in/60cm of narrow ribbon

GAUGE

23 sts and 32 rows to 4in/10cm measured over stockinette stitch using size 5 (3.75mm) needles and two strands of yarn held together *or size necessary to obtain correct gauge.*

BACK

Cast on 73 (79: 85: 91: 97) sts using size 3 (3mm) needles and yarn DOUBLE.

Row 1 (RS): K0 (1: 0: 2: 0), P0 (2: 1: 2: 2), *K3, P2, rep from * to last 3 (1: 4: 2: 0) sts, K3 (1: 3: 2: 0), P0 (0: 1: 0: 0).

Row 2: P0 (1: 0: 2: 0), K0 (2: 1: 2: 2), *P3, K2, rep from * to last 3 (1: 4: 2: 0) sts, P3 (1: 3: 2: 0), K0 (0: 1: 0: 0).

These 2 rows form rib.

Work in rib for a further 18 rows, ending with a WS row.

Change to size 5 (3.75mm) needles.

Beg with a K row, cont in St st, shaping side seams by inc 1 st at each end of 3rd and every foll 6th row to 87 (91: 97: 103: 109) sts, then on every foll 8th row until there are 91 (97: 103: 109: 115) sts.

Work even until back measures 10¼ (10½: 10½: 11: 11)in/26 (27: 27: 28: 28) cm, ending with a WS row.

Shape armholes

Bind off 4 (5: 5: 6: 6) sts at beg of next 2 rows.
83 (87: 93: 97: 103) sts.

Dec 1 st at each end of next 3 (3: 5: 5: 7) rows, then on foll 2 (3: 3: 4: 4) alt rows.
73 (75: 77: 79: 81) sts.

Cont even until armhole measures 7½ (7½: 8: 8: 8¼)in/19 (19: 20: 20: 21)cm, ending with a WS row.

Shape shoulders and back neck

Bind off 7 sts at beg of next 2 rows.
59 (61: 63: 65: 67) sts.

Next row (RS): Bind off 7 sts, K until there are 10 (10: 11: 11: 12) sts on right needle and turn, leaving rem sts on a holder.

Work each side of neck separately.

Bind off 4 sts at beg of next row.

Bind off rem 6 (6: 7: 7: 8) sts.

With RS facing, rejoin yarn to rem sts, bind off center 25 (27: 27: 29: 29) sts, K to end.

Complete to match first side, reversing shapings.

FRONT

Work as given for back until 2 rows less have been worked than on back to start of armhole shaping, ending with a WS row.

Divide for front opening

Next row (RS): K44 (47: 50: 53: 56), pick up loop lying between needles and place on right needle (**note**: this loop does NOT count as a st), sl next st knitwise and turn, leaving rem sts on a holder.

Work each side of neck separately.

Next row: P tog first st and the loop, P to end.
45 (48: 51: 54: 57) sts.

Last 2 rows set front opening edge sts.

Shape armhole

Keeping front opening edge sts correct as set, cont as foll:

Bind off 4 (5: 5: 6: 6) sts at beg of next row.
41 (43: 46: 48: 51) sts.

Work 1 row.

Dec 1 st at armhole edge of next 3 (3: 5: 5: 7) rows, then on foll 2 (3: 3: 4: 4) alt rows.
36 (37: 38: 39: 40) sts.

Cont even until 22 (22: 22: 24: 24) rows fewer have been worked than on back to start of shoulder shaping, ending with a WS row.

Shape neck

Next row (RS): K29 (29: 30: 31: 32) and turn, leaving rem 7 (8: 8: 8: 8) sts on a holder.

Work each side of neck separately.

Dec 1 st at neck edge of next 4 rows, then on foll 4 (4: 4: 5: 5) alt rows, then on foll 4th row.
20 (20: 21: 21: 22) sts.

Work 5 rows, ending with a WS row.

Shape shoulder

Bind off 7 sts at beg of next and foll alt row.

Work 1 row.

Bind off rem 6 (6: 7: 7: 8) sts.

With RS facing, rejoin yarn to rem sts, K2tog, K to end.

Next row (RS): P to last st, pick up loop lying between needles and place on right needle (**note**: this loop does NOT count as a st), sl next st purlwise.

Next row: K tog tbl first st and the loop, K to end. *45 (48: 51: 54: 57) sts.*

Last 2 rows set front opening edge sts.

Complete to match first side, reversing shapings.

SLEEVES (both alike)

Cast on 72 (74: 76: 78: 80) sts using size 3 (3mm) needles and yarn **DOUBLE**.

Row 1 (RS): K0 (1: 2: 3: 0), P2 (2: 2: 2: 1), *K3, P2, rep from * to last 0 (1: 2: 3: 4) sts, K0 (1: 2: 3: 3), P0 (0: 0: 0: 1).

Row 2: P0 (1: 2: 3: 0), K2 (2: 2: 2: 1), *P3, K2, rep from * to last 0 (1: 2: 3: 4) sts, P0 (1: 2: 3: 3), K0 (0: 0: 0: 1).

These 2 rows form rib.

Work in rib for a further 6 rows, ending with a WS row.

Change to size 5 (3.75mm) needles.

Shape top

Beg with a K row, cont in St st as foll:

Bind off 4 (5: 5: 6: 6) sts at beg of next 2 rows. *64 (64: 66: 66: 68) sts.*

Dec 1 st at each end of next 3 rows, then on foll 2 alt rows, then on every foll 4th row until 40 (40: 42: 42: 44) sts rem.

Work 1 row, ending with a WS row.

Dec 1 st at each end of next and foll 1 (1: 2: 2: 3) alt rows, then on foll row, ending with a WS row.

Bind off rem 34 sts.

FINISHING

PRESS as described on the information page 138. Join right shoulder seam using back stitch, or mattress st if preferred.

Neckband

With RS facing, using size 3 (3mm) needles and yarn DOUBLE, slip 7 (8: 8: 8: 8) sts from right front holder onto right needle, rejoin yarn and pick up and knit 24 (24: 24: 26: 26) sts up right side of neck, 31 (34: 34: 35: 35) sts from back, 24 (24: 24: 26: 26) sts down left side of neck, then patt across 7 (8: 8: 8: 8) sts from left front holder. *93 (98: 98: 103: 103) sts.*

Row 1 (WS): P tog first st and the loop, P2, *K2, P3, rep from * to last 5 sts, K2, P2, pick up loop lying between needles and place on right needle, sl last st purlwise.

Row 2: K tog tbl first st and the loop, K2, *P2, K3, rep from * to last 5 sts, P2, K2, pick up loop lying between needles and place on right needle, sl last st knitwise.

Rep last 2 rows once more.

Bind off in rib.

See information page 138 for finishing instructions, setting in sleeves using the set-in method and gathering in fullness at sleevehead as in photograph. Cut ribbon into 2 equal lengths and attach to inside of neck edge.

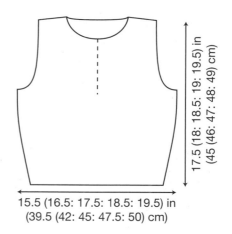

15.5 (16.5: 17.5: 18.5: 19.5) in (39.5 (42: 45: 47.5: 50) cm)

17.5 (18: 18.5: 19: 19.5) in (45 (46: 47: 48: 49) cm)

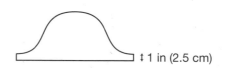

↕ 1 in (2.5 cm)

Kirk

A great chunky sweater, this design is a classic with its cable-patterned front and back and wide ribbed sleeves. The stand-up collar is zippered at the front to allow the sweater to be pulled over the head easily and also makes it easy to wear a shirt underneath it. In a chunky weight yarn, it will knit up quickly.

YARN AND SIZES

	S	M	L	XL	XXL	
To fit chest	38	40	42	44	46	in
	97	102	107	112	117	cm

Chunky (CYCA Bulky) yarn
Rowan *Cocoon* (80% merino wool, 20% kid mohair; 226yd/100g) in Quarry Tile 818

	8	8	9	9	10	balls

(Originally photographed in Rowan *Polar* Blast 654)

NEEDLES
1 pair size 10½ (7mm) needles
1 pair size 11 (8mm) needles
Cable needle

EXTRAS
Zipper to fit front opening

GAUGE
16 sts and 16 rows to 4in/10cm measured over cable and rib pattern using size 11 (8mm) needles *or size necessary to obtain correct gauge.*

YARN NOTE
This garment was knitted originally in Rowan *Polar*. We suggest you substitute Rowan *Cocoon*, which knits to a very similar gauge. However, make sure you do a gauge swatch and, if necessary, adapt your needle size (up or down) to achieve the gauge on the pattern. If you do not, even a couple of stitches/rows difference on a thick yarn over a 4in/10cm swatch will make a noticeable difference to the width/length of the garment. For further information, see page140.

SPECIAL ABBREVIATIONS
C6B = slip next 4 sts onto cable needle and leave at back of work, K2, slip the 2 P sts back onto left needle and P2, then K2 from cable needle.
C6F = slip next 4 sts onto cable needle and leave at front of work, K2, slip the 2 P sts back onto left needle and P2, then K2 from cable needle.

BACK

Cast on 92 (94: 98: 100: 104) sts using size 10½ (7mm) needles.

Row 1 (RS): K1 (0: 0: 1: 0), P2 (0: 2: 2: 1), *K2, P2, rep from * to last 1 (2: 0: 1: 3) sts, K1 (2: 0: 1: 2), P0 (0: 0: 0: 1).

Row 2: P1 (0: 0: 1: 0), K2 (0: 2: 2: 1), *P2, K2, rep from * to last 1 (2: 0: 1: 3) sts, P1 (2: 0: 1: 2), K0 (0: 0: 0: 1).

These 2 rows form rib.

Work in rib for a further 14 rows, ending with a WS row.

Change to size 11 (8mm) needles.

Cont in patt as foll:

Row 1 (RS): Rib 3 (4: 6: 7: 1), [C6F, P2] 5 (5: 5: 5: 6) times, rib 6, [P2, C6B] 5 (5: 5: 5: 6) times, rib 3 (4: 6: 7: 1).

Work in rib for 7 rows.

Row 9: Rib 7 (8: 2: 3: 5), [C6B, P2] 4 (4: 5: 5: 5) times, C6B, P2, C6F, [P2, C6F] 4 (4: 5: 5: 5) times, rib 7 (8: 2: 3: 5).

Work in rib for 7 rows.

These 16 rows form patt.

Cont in patt until back measures 17 (17: 17½: 17½: 17¾)in/43 (43: 44: 44: 45)cm, ending with a WS row.

Shape armholes

Keeping patt correct, bind off 5 (6: 8: 5: 7) sts at beg of next 2 rows. *82 (82: 82: 90: 90) sts.*

Next row (RS): P2, K2, P1, P2tog tbl, patt to last 7 sts, P2tog, P1, K2, P2.

Next row: K2, P2, K1, K2tog, patt to last 7 sts, K2tog tbl, K1, P2, K2.

Rep last 2 rows 1 (1: 1: 3: 3) times more. *74 sts.*

Next row (RS): P2, K2, P1, P2tog tbl, patt to last 7 sts, P2tog, P1, K2, P2.

Next row: K2, P2, K2, patt to last 6 sts, K2, P2, K2.

Rep last 2 rows 3 times more. *66 sts.*

Cont even until armhole measures 8¾ (9: 9: 9½: 9½)in/22 (23: 23: 24: 24)cm, ending with a WS row.

Shape shoulders and back neck

Bind off 6 sts at beg of next 2 rows. *54 sts.*

Next row (RS): Bind off 6 sts, patt until there are 10 sts on right needle and turn, leaving rem sts on a holder.

Work each side of neck separately.

Bind off 4 sts at beg of next row.

Bind off rem 6 sts.

With RS facing, rejoin yarn to rem sts, bind off center 22 sts, patt to end.

Complete to match first side, reversing shapings.

FRONT

Work as given for back to beg of armhole shaping, ending with a WS row.

Shape armhole and divide for front opening

Next row (RS): Bind off 5 (6: 8: 5: 7) sts, patt until there are 41 (41: 41: 45: 45) sts on right needle and turn, leaving rem sts on a holder.

Work each side of neck separately.

Work 1 row.

Next row (RS): P2, K2, P1, P2tog tbl, patt to end.

Next row: Patt to last 7 sts, K2tog tbl, K1, P2, K2.

Rep last 2 rows 1 (1: 1: 3: 3) times more. *37 sts.*

Next row (RS): P2, K2, P1, P2tog tbl, patt to end.

Next row: Patt to last 6 sts, K2, P2, K2.

Rep last 2 rows 3 times more. *33 sts.*

Cont even until 12 rows fewer have been worked than on back to start of shoulder shaping, ending with a WS row.

Shape neck

Next row (RS): Patt to last 9 sts and turn, leaving rem 9 sts on a holder. *24 sts.*

Dec 1 st at neck edge of next 4 rows, then on foll alt row, then on foll 4th row. *18 sts.*

Work 1 row, ending with a WS row.

Shape shoulder

Bind off 6 sts at beg of next and foll alt row.

Work 1 row. Bind off rem 6 sts.

With RS facing, rejoin yarn to rem sts, patt to end. Complete to match first side, reversing shapings and working first row of neck shaping as foll:

Next row (RS): Patt 9 sts and slip these 9 sts onto a holder, patt to end. *24 sts.*

SLEEVES (both alike)

Cast on 34 sts using size 10½ (7mm) needles.

Row 1 (RS): P2, *K2, P2, rep from * to end.

Row 2: K2, *P2, K2, rep from * to end.

These 2 rows form rib.

Work in rib for a further 6 rows, ending with a WS row.

Change to size 11 (8mm) needles.

Row 9 (RS): Rib 6, C6B, rib 10, C6F, rib 6.

Work in rib for 7 rows.

Row 17: Inc in first st, rib 9, C6B, P2, C6F, rib 9, inc in last st. *36 sts.*

Work in rib for 7 rows, inc 1 st at each end of 6th (6th: 4th: 4th: 4th) of these rows. *38 sts.*

Row 25: [Inc in first st] 0 (0: 1: 1: 1) times, rib 8 (8: 7: 7: 7), C6B, rib 10, C6F, rib 8 (8: 7: 7: 7), [inc in last st] 0 (0: 1: 1: 1) times. *38 (38: 40: 40: 40) sts.*

Cont in rib, shaping sides by inc 1 st at each end of 6th (4th: 6th: 4th: 4th) and every foll 8th (6th: 6th: 4th: 4th) row to 50 (44: 56: 44: 56) sts, then on every foll - (8th: -: 6th: 6th) row until there are - (52: -: 58: 62) sts, taking inc sts into rib.

Cont even until sleeve measures 19¼ (19¾: 19¾: 20: 20)in/49 (50: 50: 51: 51)cm, ending with a WS row.

Shape top

Keeping rib correct, bind off 4 (5: 7: 4: 6) sts at beg of next 2 rows. *42 (42: 42: 50: 50) sts.*

Next row (RS): P2, K2, P1, P2tog tbl, rib to last 7 sts, P2tog, P1, K2, P2.

Next row: K2, P2, K1, K2tog, rib to last 7 sts, K2tog tbl, K1, P2, K2.

Rep last 2 rows 0 (0: 0: 2: 2) times more. *38 sts.*

Next row: P2, K2, P1, P2tog tbl, rib to last 7 sts,

Special tip

INSERTING A ZIPPER

The key to successfully inserting a zipper into a knitted opening is to work slowly and carefully. Start by basting together the opening edges so that they butt up against each other and the upper, bound-off edges (and any pattern details, such as pick-up rows) match. Lay the knitted opening over the closed zipper so that the zipper teeth are directly underneath the basted-together edges, and position the top of the zipper pull just below the upper (bound-off) edges. Taking great care NOT to stretch the knitting, baste the zipper in place along both edges of the opening. Using a matching shade of sewing thread and back stitch, sew the zipper in place by stitching through both the knitting and the zipper tapes, stitching approx $^3/_8$in/8mm in from the knitted opening edges. Work slowly and carefully, taking care not to stretch the knitting. You will find that the back stitches will virtually disappear into the knitting. Once the zipper is in place, remove all the basting threads. Fold the upper ends of the zipper tapes back on themselves on the inside, folding them at a slight angle so as not to interfere with the zipper teeth, and slip stitch to the knitting. You can also slip stitch the outer edges of the zipper tapes in place too—this will make the opening much neater if the zipper is left open and the tapes are visible.

P2tog, P1, K2, P2.
Next row: K2, P2, K2, rib to last 6 sts, K2, P2, K2.
Rep last 2 rows once more. *34 sts.*
Next row: P2, K2, P1, P2tog tbl, rib to last 7 sts, P2tog, P1, K2, P2.
Next row: K2, P2, K2, rib to last 6 sts, K2, P2, K2.
Next row: P2, K2, P2, rib to last 6 sts, P2, K2, P2.
Next row: K2, P2, K2, rib to last 6 sts, K2, P2, K2.
Rep last 4 rows twice more. *28 sts.*
Next row: P2, K2, P1, P2tog tbl, rib to last 7 sts, P2tog, P1, K2, P2. *26 sts.*
Next row: K2, P2, K2, rib to last 6 sts, K2, P2, K2.
Next row: P2, K2, P1, P2tog tbl, rib to last 7 sts, P2tog, P1, K2, P2.
Next row: K2, P2, K1, K2tog, rib to last 7 sts, K2tog tbl, K1, P2, K2.
Rep last 2 rows once more.
Bind off rem 18 sts.

FINISHING

PRESS as described on the information page 138. Join both shoulder seams using back stitch, or mattress stitch if preferred.

Collar

With RS facing and using size 10½ (7mm) needles, slip 9 sts from right front onto right needle, rejoin yarn and pick up and knit 12 sts up right side of neck, 22 sts from back, and 12 sts down left side of neck, then patt 9 sts from left front holder. *64 sts.*
Cont in rib as set by sts left on holders until collar measures 3½in/9cm.
Bind off in rib.
See information page 138 for finishing instructions, setting in sleeves using the set-in method. Insert zipper into front opening (see tip).

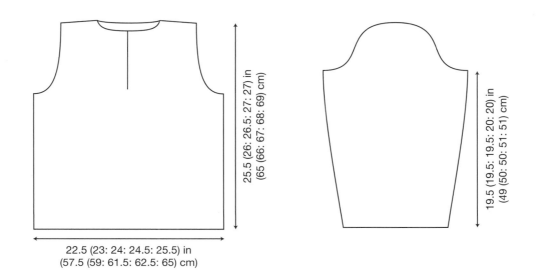

25.5 (26: 26.5: 27: 27) in
(65 (66: 67: 68: 69) cm)

22.5 (23: 24: 24.5: 25.5) in
(57.5 (59: 61.5: 62.5: 65) cm)

19.5 (19.5: 19.5: 20: 20) in
(49 (50: 50: 51: 51) cm)

Iris

This simple shrug was a trendsetter, well ahead of its time. Knitted in Rowan *Calmer* (a relatively thick cotton blend yarn), it comes in two versions, one with a long sleeve and the other with a three-quarter sleeve. You can fasten the shrug at the front with either a brooch or with leather thonging threaded through the eyelet holes.

YARN

	XS	S	M	L	XL	
To fit bust	32	34	36	38	40	in
	81	86	91	97	102	cm

Aran (CYCA Medium) yarn
Rowan *Calmer* (75% cotton, 25% acrylic microfiber; 175yd/50g)
Long sleeve version in Drift 460

	5	5	5	6	6	balls

Three-quarter sleeve version in Slosh 479

	5	5	5	5	6	balls

(Originally photographed in Joy 478)

NEEDLES
1 pair size 7 (4.5mm) needles
1 pair size 8 (5mm) needles

EXTRAS
31$\frac{1}{2}$in/80cm of leather thonging

GAUGE
21 sts and 30 rows to 4in/10cm measured over stockinette stitch using size 8 (5mm) needles *or size necessary to obtain correct gauge.*

Pattern note: As row end edges of fronts form actual finished edges of garment it is important these edges are kept neat. Therefore all new balls of yarn should be joined in at side seam or armhole edges of rows.

BACK

Cast on 76 (82: 88: 94: 100) sts using size 7 (4.5mm) needles.

Work in garter st for 4 rows, ending with a WS row.

Change to size 8 (5mm) needles.

Beg with a K row, work in St st for 8 rows.

Row 9 (RS): K3, M1, K to last 3 sts, M1, K3.

Working all increases as set by last row, inc 1 st at each end of every foll 8th row until there are 84 (90: 96: 102: 108) sts.

Work 13 rows, ending with a WS row. (Back should measure 6¼in/16cm.)

Shape armholes

Bind off 3 (4: 4: 5: 5) sts at beg of next 2 rows. *78 (82: 88: 92: 98) sts.*

Next row (RS): K3, K2tog, K to last 5 sts, K2tog tbl, K3.

Next row: P3, P2tog tbl, P to last 5 sts, P2tog, P3.

Working all decreases as set by last 2 rows, dec 1 st at each end of next 1 (1: 3: 3: 5) rows, then on foll 3 (4: 4: 5: 5) alt rows. *66 (68: 70: 72: 74) sts.*

Cont even until armhole measures 7½ (7½: 8: 8: 8¼)in/19 (19: 20: 20: 21)cm, ending with a WS row.

Shape shoulders and back neck

Bind off 6 (6: 6: 6: 7) sts at beg of next 2 rows. *54 (56: 58: 60: 60) sts.*

Next row (RS): Bind off 6 (6: 6: 6: 7) sts, K until there are 10 (10: 11: 11: 10) sts on right needle and turn, leaving rem sts on a holder.

Work each side of neck separately.

Bind off 4 sts at beg of next row.

Bind off rem 6 (6: 7: 7: 6) sts.

With RS facing, rejoin yarn to rem sts, bind off center 22 (24: 24: 26: 26) sts, K to end.

Complete to match first side, reversing shapings.

LEFT FRONT

Cast on 35 (38: 41: 44: 47) sts using size 7

(4.5mm) needles.

Work in garter st for 4 rows, inc 1 st at beg of 2nd row and at same edge on foll 2 rows and ending with a WS row. *38 (41: 44: 47: 50) sts.*

Change to size 8 (5mm) needles.

Row 1 (RS): K4 (7: 10: 13: 16), wrap next st (by slipping next st onto right needle, bringing yarn to front (RS) of work between needles and then slipping same st back onto left needle—on foll rows, Ktog the loop and the wrapped st) and turn.

Row 2 and every foll alt row: Purl.

Row 3: K9 (12: 15: 18: 21), wrap next st and turn.

Row 5: K13 (16: 19: 22: 25), wrap next st and turn.

Row 7: K16 (19: 22: 25: 28), wrap next st and turn.

Row 9: K3, M1, K16 (19: 22: 25: 28), wrap next st and turn.

Row 11: K23 (26: 29: 32: 35), wrap next st and turn.

Row 13: K25 (28: 31: 34: 37), wrap next st and turn.

Row 15: K27 (30: 33: 36: 39), wrap next st and turn.

Row 17: K3, M1, K26 (29: 32: 35: 38), wrap next st and turn.

Row 19: K32 (35: 38: 41: 44), wrap next st and turn.

Row 21: K34 (37: 40: 43: 46), wrap next st and turn.

Row 23: K36 (39: 42: 45: 48), wrap next st and turn.

Row 25: K3, M1, K34 (37: 40: 43: 46), wrap next st and turn.

Row 27: K39 (42: 45: 48: 51), wrap next st and turn.

Row 29: K40 (43: 46: 49: 52), wrap next st and turn.

Row 30: Purl.

Row 31: K to last st, pick up loop lying between needles and place this loop on right needle (**note:** this loop does NOT count as a st), slip last st knitwise.

Row 32: P tog first st and the loop, P to end.
Last 2 rows form St st with front opening edge
sl st edging.
Keeping sl st edging correct, cont as foll:
Row 33 (RS): K3, M1, K to last 4 sts, K2tog tbl, yo
(to form eyelet), patt 2 sts. *42 (45: 48: 51: 54) sts.*
Work 5 rows, ending with a WS row.

Shape front slope
Next row (RS): K to last 16 sts, K2tog tbl, patt to
end. *41 (44: 47: 50: 53) sts.*
Working all front slope shaping as set by last row,
cont as foll:
Work 7 rows, dec 1 st at front slope edge on 4th of
these rows. *40 (43: 46: 49: 52) sts.*

Shape armhole
Bind off 3 (4: 4: 5: 5) sts at beg and dec 1 st at
front slope edge of next row. *36 (38: 41: 43: 46) sts.*
Work 1 row.
Next row (RS): K3, K2tog, patt to end.
Next row: Patt to last 5 sts, P2tog, P3.
Working all decreases as set by last 2 rows, dec 1
st at armhole edge of next 1 (1: 3: 3: 5) rows, then
on foll 3 (4: 4: 5: 5) alt rows **and at same time** dec
1 st at front slope edge of next and every foll 4th
row. *28 (28: 29: 29: 30) sts.*
Dec 1 st at front slope edge **only** on 2nd (4th: 2nd:
4th: 2nd) and every foll 4th row until 19 (19: 20:
20: 21) sts rem.
Cont even until left front matches back to start of
shoulder shaping, ending with a WS row.

Shape shoulder
Bind off 6 (6: 6: 6: 7) sts at beg of next and foll alt
row.
Work 1 row. Bind off rem 7 (7: 8: 8: 7) sts.

RIGHT FRONT
Cast on 35 (38: 41: 44: 47) sts using size 7
(4.5mm) needles.
Work in garter st for 4 rows, inc 1 st at end of 2nd
row and at same edge on foll 2 rows and ending

with a WS row. *38 (41: 44: 47: 50) sts.*
Change to size 8 (5mm) needles.
Row 1 and every foll alt row except rows 9, 17, and 25: Knit.
Row 2 (WS): P4 (7: 10: 13: 16), wrap next st (by slipping next st onto right needle, taking yarn to back (RS) of work between needles and then slipping same st back onto left needle—on foll rows, P tog the loop and the wrapped st) and turn.
Row 4: P9 (12: 15: 18: 21), wrap next st and turn.
Row 6: P13 (16: 19: 22: 25), wrap next st and turn.
Row 8: P16 (19: 22: 25: 28), wrap next st and turn.
Row 9: K to last 3 sts, M1, K3.
Row 10: P20 (23: 26: 29: 32), wrap next st and turn.
Row 12: P23 (26: 29: 32: 35), wrap next st and turn.
Row 14: P25 (28: 31: 34: 37), wrap next st and turn.
Row 16: P27 (30: 33: 36: 39), wrap next st and turn.

Row 17: As row 9.
Row 18: P30 (33: 36: 39: 42), wrap next st and turn.
Row 20: P32 (35: 38: 41: 44), wrap next st and turn.
Row 22: P34 (37: 40: 43: 46), wrap next st and turn.
Row 24: P36 (39: 42: 45: 48), wrap next st and turn.
Row 25: As row 9.
Row 26: P38 (41: 44: 47: 50), wrap next st and turn.
Row 28: P39 (42: 45: 48: 51), wrap next st and turn.
Row 30: P40 (43: 46: 49: 52), wrap next st and turn.
Row 31: Knit.
Row 32: P to last st, pick up loop lying between needles and place this loop on right needle (**note**: this loop does NOT count as a st), slip last st purlwise.
Row 33: K tog tbl first st and the loop, K1, yo, K2tog (to form eyelet), K to last 3 sts, M1, K3.
42 (45: 48: 51: 54) sts.
Last 2 rows form St st with front opening edge sl st edging.
Keeping sl st edging correct, cont as foll:
Work 5 rows, ending with a WS row.
Shape front slope
Next row (RS): Patt 14 sts, K2tog, K to end.
41 (44: 47: 50: 53) sts.
Working all front slope shaping as set by last row and all armhole shaping as set by back, complete to match left front, reversing shapings.

LONG SLEEVES (both alike)
Cast on 46 (46: 48: 50: 50) sts using size 7 (4.5mm) needles.
Work in garter st for 4 rows, ending with a WS row.
Change to size 8 (5mm) needles.
Beg with a K row, work in St st for 6 rows.
Next row (RS): K3, M1, K to last 3 sts, M1, K3.
Working all increases as set by last row, inc 1 st at each end of every foll 12th (12th: 12th: 12th: 10th) row to 62 (52: 58: 60: 72) sts, then on every foll 10th (10th: 10th: 10th: 8th) row until there are 66 (68: 70: 72: 74) sts.

Cont even until sleeve measures 17 (17: 17$\frac{1}{2}$: 17$\frac{1}{2}$: 17$\frac{1}{2}$)in/43 (43: 44: 44: 44)cm, ending with a WS row.

Shape top
Bind off 3 (4: 4: 5: 5) sts at beg of next 2 rows.
60 (60: 62: 62: 64) sts.
Dec 1 st at each end of next 3 rows, then on foll 5 alt rows, then on every foll 4th row until 34 (34: 36: 36: 38) sts rem.
Work 1 row, ending with a WS row.
Dec 1 st at each end of next and every foll alt row to 30 sts, then on foll 3 rows, ending with a WS row.
Bind off rem 24 sts.

THREE-QUARTER LENGTH SLEEVES (both alike)
Cast on 52 (52: 54: 56: 56) sts using size 7 (4.5mm) needles.
Work in garter st for 4 rows, ending with a WS row.
Change to size 8 (5mm) needles.
Beg with a K row, work in St st for 6 rows.
Next row (RS): K3, M1, K to last 3 sts, M1, K3.
Working all increases as set by last row, inc 1 st at

each end of every foll 14th (12th: 12th: 12th: 10th) row to 56 (58: 64: 66: 72) sts, then on every foll 12th (10th: 10th: 10th: 8th) row until there are 66 (68: 70: 72: 74) sts.
Cont even until sleeve measures 13 (13: 13$\frac{1}{2}$: 13$\frac{1}{2}$: 13$\frac{1}{2}$)in/33 (33: 34: 34: 34)cm, ending with a WS row. Complete as given for long sleeves from start of sleeve top shaping.

FINISHING
PRESS as described on the information page 138.
Back neck edging
With RS facing and using size 7 (4.5mm) needles, pick up and knit 30 (32: 32: 34: 34) sts from back neck edge. Bind off knitwise (on WS).
Join both shoulder seams using back stitch, or mattress stitch if preferred.
See information page 138 for finishing instructions, setting in sleeves using the set-in method. Thread thonging through eyelet holes.

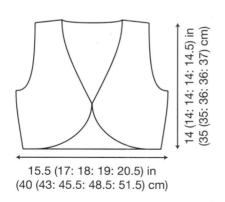

14 (14: 14: 14: 14.5) in (35 (35: 36: 36: 37) cm)

15.5 (17: 18: 19: 20.5) in (40 (43: 45.5: 48.5: 51.5) cm)

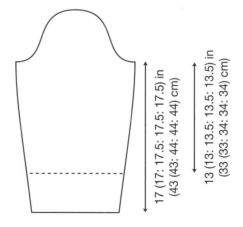

17 (17: 17.5: 17.5: 17.5) in (43 (43: 44: 44: 44) cm)

13 (13: 13.5: 13.5: 13.5) in (33 (33: 34: 34: 34) cm)

Finn & Edda

These two jackets were created as a his and hers set, but knitted in different yarns. Finn is knitted in thick *Felted Tweed Aran* and Edda is knitted in softer but also thick *Kid Classic*. The Finn design features deep ribbed welt and cuffs, plus a broad ribbed button band. Edda is knitted in rib, to create a figure-hugging style.

YARN AND SIZES (FINN)

	S	M	L	XL	XXL	
To fit chest	38	40	42	44	46	in
	97	102	107	112	117	cm

Aran (CYCA Medium) yarn
Rowan *Felted Tweed Aran* (50% merino wool, 25% alpaca, 15% viscose; 95yd/50g) in Pebble 720

	11	12	13	13	14	balls

(Originally photographed in Rowan *Yorkshire Tweed Aran* in Tusk 417)

NEEDLES AND EXTRAS

1 pair size 6 (4mm) needles; 1 pair size 7 (4.5mm) needles; 1 pair size 8 (5mm) needles
Buttons: 7 x Rowan 00343

GAUGE

16 sts and 23 rows to 4in/10cm measured over stockinette stitch using size 8 (5mm) needles *or size necessary to obtain correct gauge.*

YARN AND SIZES (EDDA)

	XS	S	M	L	XL	
To fit bust	32	34	36	38	40	in
	81	86	91	97	102	cm

Worsted (CYCA Medium) yarn
Rowan *Kid Classic* (70% lambswool, 25% kid mohair, 4% nylon; 153yd/50g) in Cherry Red 847

	8	8	9	9	10	balls

NEEDLES AND EXTRAS

1 pair size 10 (6mm) needles, 1 pair size 10½ (7mm) needles; Buttons: 4 x Rowan 00348

GAUGE

22 sts and 28 rows to 4in/10cm measured over pattern using size 10½ (7mm) needles *or size necessary to obtain correct gauge.*

YARN NOTE

Finn was knitted originally in Rowan *Yorkshire Tweed Aran*. We suggest you substitute Rowan *Felted Tweed Aran*, which knits to a very similar gauge. However, make sure you do a gauge swatch and, if necessary, adapt your needle size (up or down) to achieve the gauge on the pattern. For further information, see page 140.

Finn

BACK

Lower section

Cast on 89 (93: 97: 101: 105) sts using size 7 (4.5mm) needles.

Row 1 (RS): P0 (2: 0: 2: 0), *K1, P3, rep from * to last 1 (3: 1: 3: 1) sts, K1, P0 (2: 0: 2: 0).

Row 2: K0 (2: 0: 2: 0), *P1, K3, rep from * to last 1 (3: 1: 3: 1) sts, P1, K0 (2: 0: 2: 0).

These 2 rows form rib.

Work in rib for a further 38 rows, ending with a WS row.

Bind off in rib.

Main section

With WS facing (so that ridge is formed on RS of work) and using size 8 (5mm) needles, pick up and knit 89 (93: 97: 101: 105) sts across bound-off edge of lower section.

Beg with a K row, cont in St st until back measures 15½in/39cm from cast-on edge of lower section, ending with a WS row.

Shape raglan armholes

Bind off 6 sts at beg of next 2 rows.
77 (81: 85: 89: 93) sts.

Next row (RS): K1, K2tog, K to last 3 sts, K2tog tbl, K1.

Next row: [P1, P2tog tbl] 0 (0: 1: 1: 1) times, P to last 0 (0: 3: 3: 3) sts, [P2tog, P1] 0 (0: 1: 1: 1) times.

Working all decreases as set by last 2 rows, dec 1 st at each end of next and every foll alt row until 23 (25: 25: 27: 29) sts rem, ending with a RS row.

Next row: P1, P2tog tbl, P to last 3 sts, P2tog, P1.

Bind off rem 21 (23: 23: 25: 27) sts.

LEFT FRONT

Lower section

Cast on 37 (39: 41: 43: 45) sts using size 7 (4.5mm) needles.

Row 1 (RS): P0 (2: 0: 2: 0), *K1, P3, rep from * to last st, K1.

Row 2: *P1, K3, rep from * to last 1 (3: 1: 3: 1) sts, P1, K0 (2: 0: 2: 0).
These 2 rows form rib.
Work in rib for a further 38 rows, ending with a WS row.
Bind off in rib.

Main section
With WS facing (so that ridge is formed on RS of work) and using size 8 (5mm) needles, pick up and knit 37 (39: 41: 43: 45) sts across bound-off edge of lower section.
Beg with a K row, cont in St st until left front matches back to beg of raglan armhole shaping, ending with a WS row.

Shape raglan armhole
Bind off 6 sts at beg of next row.
31 (33: 35: 37: 39) sts.
Work 1 row.
Working all raglan decreases as for back, dec 1 st at raglan armhole edge of next 1 (1: 3: 3: 3) rows, then on every foll alt row until 9 (10: 11: 12: 13) sts rem, ending with a RS row.

Shape neck
Bind off 1 (2: 1: 2: 3) sts at beg of next row.
8 (8: 10: 10: 10) sts.
Dec 1 st at neck edge of next 3 rows, then on foll 0 (0: 1: 1: 1) alt row **and at same time** dec 1 st at raglan armhole edge of next and foll 2 (2: 3: 3: 3) alt rows. *2 sts.*
Work 1 row.
Next row (RS): K2tog and fasten off.

RIGHT FRONT
Lower section
Cast on 37 (39: 41: 43: 45) sts using size 7 (4.5mm) needles.
Row 1 (RS): *K1, P3, rep from * to last 1 (3: 1: 3: 1) sts, K1, P0 (2: 0: 2: 0).
Row 2: K0 (2: 0: 2: 0), *P1, K3, rep from * to last st, P1.

These 2 rows form rib.
Work in rib for a further 38 rows, ending with a WS row.
Bind off in rib.

Main section
With WS facing (so that ridge is formed on RS of work) and using size 8 (5mm) needles, pick up and knit 37 (39: 41: 43: 45) sts across bound-off edge of lower section.
Beg with a K row, cont in St st and complete to match left front, reversing shapings.

SLEEVES
Lower section
Cast on 51 (51: 53: 55: 55) sts using size 7 (4.5mm) needles.
Row 1 (RS): P1 (1: 2: 3: 3), *K1, P3, rep from * to last 2 (2: 3: 4: 4) sts, K1, P1 (1: 2: 3: 3).
Row 2: K1 (1: 2: 3: 3), *P1, K3, rep from * to last 2 (2: 3: 4: 4) sts, P1, K1 (1: 2: 3: 3).
These 2 rows form rib.
Cont in rib, inc 1 st at each end of 17th and every foll 8th row until there are 57 (57: 59: 61: 61) sts, taking inc sts into rib.
Work a further 5 rows, ending with a WS row. (40 rows of rib completed.)
Bind off in rib.

Main section
With WS facing (so that ridge is formed on RS of work) and using size 8 (5mm) needles, pick up and knit 57 (57: 59: 61: 61) sts across bound-off edge of lower section.
Beg with a K row, cont in St st, shaping sides by inc 1 st at each end of 3rd and every foll 8th row to 71 (67: 69: 73: 67) sts, then on every foll 6th row until there are 75 (77: 79: 81: 83) sts.
Cont even until sleeve measures 19¼ (19¾: 19¾: 20: 20)in/49 (50: 50: 51: 51)cm from cast-on edge of lower section, ending with a WS row.

Shape raglan

Bind off 6 sts at beg of next 2 rows.
63 (65: 67: 69: 71) sts.
Next row (RS): K1, K2tog, K to last 3 sts, K2tog tbl, K1.
Next row: Purl.
Working all decreases as set by last 2 rows, dec 1 st at each end of next and every foll alt row until 13 sts rem, ending with a WS row.
Left sleeve only
Dec 1 st at each end of next row, then bind off 3 sts at beg of foll row. *8 sts.*
Dec 1 st at beg of next row, then bind off 4 sts at beg of foll row.
Right sleeve only
Bind off 4 sts at beg and dec 1 st at end of next row. *8 sts.*
Work 1 row.
Rep last 2 rows once more.
Both sleeves
Bind off rem 3 sts.

FINISHING
PRESS as described on the information page 138.
With WS together (so that seam shows on RS), join raglan seams using back stitch, or mattress stitch if preferred.
Collar
With RS facing and using size 6 (4mm) needles, starting and ending at front opening edges, pick up and knit 7 (8: 9: 10: 11) sts up right side of neck, 9 sts from right sleeve, 21 (23: 23: 25: 27) sts from back, 9 sts from left sleeve, then 7 (8: 9: 10: 11) sts down left side of neck.
53 (57: 59: 63: 67) sts.
Row 1 (WS): K1, *P1, K1, rep from * to end.
Row 2: P1, *K1, P1, rep from * to end.
These 2 rows form rib.
Cont in rib until collar measures 3in/8cm.
Bind off in rib.
Button band

With RS facing and using size 6 (4mm) needles, pick up and knit 105 (107: 109: 111: 113) sts evenly along entire right front opening edge, between cast-on edge of lower section and bound-off edge of collar.
Work in rib as given for collar for 2³/₄in/7cm.
Bind off in rib.

Buttonhole band
Work to match button band, picking up sts along left front opening edge and with the addition of 7 buttonholes worked when band measures 2in/5cm as foll:

Buttonhole row (RS): Rib 4 (2: 3: 2: 3), work 2 tog, yo (to make a buttonhole), rib 12, *work 2 tog, yo, rib 14 (15: 15: 16: 16), rep from * 4 times more, work 2 tog, yo (to make 7th buttonhole), rib to end.
See information page 138 for finishing instructions.

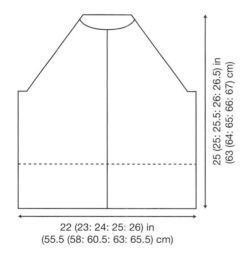

25 (25: 25.5: 26: 26.5) in
(63 (64: 65: 66: 67) cm)

22 (23: 24: 25: 26) in
(55.5 (58: 60.5: 63: 65.5) cm)

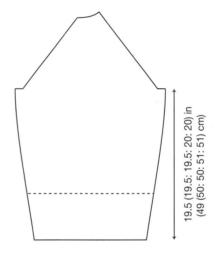

19.5 (19.5: 19.5: 20: 20) in
(49 (50: 50: 51: 51) cm)

Edda

BACK

Cast on 89 (95: 101: 107: 113) sts using size 10 (6mm) needles.

Row 1 (WS): K1, *P1, K1, rep from * to end.

Row 2: K1, *slip next st purlwise with yarn at back (WS) of work, K1, rep from * to end.

These 2 rows form patt.

Work in patt for a further 3 rows, ending with a WS row.

Change to size 10½ (7mm) needles.

Work a further 12 rows, ending with a WS row.

Counting in from both ends of last row, place markers on 20th (22nd: 24th: 26th: 28th) st in from both ends of last row.

Row 18 (dec) (RS): K2tog, patt to within 1 st of first marker, K3tog, patt to within 1 st of second marker, K3tog tbl, patt to last 2 sts, K2tog.
83 (89: 95: 101: 107) sts.

Work 9 rows.

Row 28 (dec) (RS): Patt to within 1 st of first marker, K3tog, patt to within 1 st of second marker, K3tog tbl, patt to end.
79 (85: 91: 97: 103) sts.

Work 9 rows.

Row 38: As row 18. *73 (79: 85: 91: 97) sts.*

Work 13 rows, ending with a WS row.

Row 52 (inc) (RS): Inc in first st, patt to first marked st, pick up loop lying between needles and K into back then P into front of this loop, slip marked st purlwise with yarn at back (WS) of work, patt to next marked st, slip marked st purlwise with yarn at back (WS) of work, pick up loop lying between needles and P into back then K into front of this loop, patt to last st, inc in last st.
79 (85: 91: 97: 103) sts.

Work 7 rows.

Row 60 (inc) (RS): Inc in first st, patt to last st, inc in last st. *81 (87: 93: 99: 105) sts.*

Work 7 rows.

Rep last 16 rows once more, then rows 52 to 60 again. *97 (103: 109: 115: 121) sts.*

Cont even until back measures 13¾ (14¼: 14¼: 14½: 14½)in/35 (36: 36: 37: 37)cm, ending with a WS row.

Shape armholes

Keeping patt correct, bind off 3 (4: 4: 5: 5) sts at beg of next 2 rows. *91 (95: 101: 105: 111) sts.*

Dec 1 st at each end of next 5 (5: 7: 7: 9) rows, then on foll 3 (4: 4: 5: 5) alt rows, then on foll 4th row. *73 (75: 77: 79: 81) sts.*

Cont even until armhole measures 8 (8: 8¼: 8¼: 8¾)in/20 (20: 21: 21: 22)cm, ending with a WS row.

Shape shoulders and back neck

Bind off 7 (7: 8: 8: 8) sts at beg of next 2 rows. *59 (61: 61: 63: 65) sts.*

Next row (RS): Bind off 7 (7: 8: 8: 8) sts, patt until there are 12 (12: 11: 11: 12) sts on right needle and turn, leaving rem sts on a holder.

Work each side of neck separately.

Bind off 4 sts at beg of next row.

Bind off rem 8 (8: 7: 7: 8) sts.

With RS facing, rejoin yarn to rem sts, bind off center 21 (23: 23: 25: 25) sts, patt to end.

Complete to match first side, reversing shapings.

LEFT FRONT

Cast on 51 (53: 57: 59: 63) sts using size 10 (6mm) needles.

Work in patt as given for back for 5 rows, ending with a WS row.

Change to size 10½ (7mm) needles.

Work a further 12 rows, ending with a WS row.

Counting in from end of last row, place marker on 20th (22nd: 24th: 26th: 28th) st in from end of last row.

Row 18 (dec) (RS): K2tog, patt to within 1 st of marker, K3tog, patt to end. *48 (50: 54: 56: 60) sts.*

Work 9 rows.

Row 28 (dec) (RS): Patt to within 1 st of marker, K3tog, patt to end. *46 (48: 52: 54: 58) sts.*

Work 9 rows.

Row 38: As row 18. *43 (45: 49: 51: 55) sts.*

Work 13 rows, ending with a WS row.

Row 52 (inc) (RS): Inc in first st, patt to marked st, pick up loop lying between needles and K into back then P into front of this loop, slip marked st purlwise with yarn at back (WS) of work, patt to end. *46 (48: 52: 54: 58) sts.*

Work 7 rows.

Row 60 (inc) (RS): Inc in first st, patt to end. *47 (49: 53: 55: 59) sts.*

Work 7 rows.

Rep last 16 rows once more, then rows 52 to 60 again. *55 (57: 61: 63: 67) sts.*

Cont even until left front matches back to beg of armhole shaping, ending with a WS row.

Shape armhole and lapel

Next row (RS): Bind off 3 (4: 4: 5: 5) sts, patt to last 3 sts, pick up loop lying between needles and K into back then P into front of this loop, patt 3 sts. *54 (55: 59: 60: 64) sts.*

This row sets lapel increases at front opening edge.

Work 1 row.

Dec 1 st at armhole edge of next 5 (5: 7: 7: 9) rows, then on foll 3 (4: 4: 5: 5) alt rows, then on foll 4th row **and at same time** inc 2 sts at front opening edge on 13th row. *47 (47: 49: 49: 51) sts.*

Inc 2 sts at front opening edge of 12th (10th: 8th: 6th: 4th) row. *49 (49: 51: 51: 53) sts.*

Cont even until 13 (13: 13: 15: 15) rows less have been worked than on back to start of shoulder shaping, ending with a RS row.

Shape neck

Keeping patt correct, bind off 21 (21: 22: 21: 22) sts at beg of next row. *28 (28: 29: 30: 31) sts.*

Place marker on last bound-off st of last row.

Dec 1 st at neck edge of next and foll 5 (5: 5: 6: 6) alt rows. *22 (22: 23: 23: 24) sts.*

Work 1 row, ending with a WS row.

Shape shoulder

Bind off 7 (7: 8: 8: 8) sts at beg of next and foll alt row.

Work 1 row.

Bind off rem 8 (8: 7: 7: 8) sts.

Mark positions for 4 buttons along left front opening edge—first to come in row 22, last to come 1½in/4cm below beg of armhole and lapel shaping, and rem 2 buttons evenly spaced between.

RIGHT FRONT

Cast on 51 (53: 57: 59: 63) sts using size 10 (6mm) needles.

Work in patt as given for back for 5 rows, ending with a WS row.

Change to size 10½ (7mm) needles.

Work a further 12 rows, ending with a WS row.

Counting in from beg of last row, place marker on 20th (22nd: 24th: 26th: 28th) st in from beg of last row.

Row 18 (dec) (RS): Patt to within 1 st of marker, K3tog tbl, patt to last 2 sts, K2tog.
48 (50: 54: 56: 60) sts.

Work 3 rows, ending with a WS row.

Row 22 (buttonhole row) (RS): Patt 4 sts, yo, K2tog, patt to end.

Working a further 3 buttonholes in this way to correspond with positions marked for buttons on left front and noting that no further reference will be made to buttonholes, cont as foll:

Work a further 5 rows.

Row 28 (dec) (RS): Patt to within 1 st of marker, K3tog tbl, patt to end. *46 (48: 52: 54: 58) sts.*

Work 9 rows.

Row 38: As row 18. *43 (45: 49: 51: 55) sts.*

Work 13 rows, ending with a WS row.

Row 52 (inc) (RS): Patt to marked st, slip marked st purlwise with yarn at back (WS) of work, pick up loop lying between needles and P into back then K into front of this loop, patt to last st, inc in last st. *46 (48: 52: 54: 58) sts.*

Complete to match left front, reversing shapings.

SLEEVES (both alike)

Cast on 57 (57: 59: 61: 61) sts using size 10 (6mm) needles.

Work in patt as given for back for 5 rows, ending with a WS row.

Change to size 10¹/₂ (7mm) needles.

Cont in patt, shaping sides by inc 1 st at each end of 15th and every foll 16th (14th: 14th: 14th: 12th) row to 63 (69: 67: 69: 71) sts, then on every foll 18th (16th: 16th: 16th: 14th) row until there are 69 (71: 73: 75: 77) sts, taking inc sts into patt.

Cont even until sleeve measures 17 (17: 17¹/₂: 17¹/₂: 17¹/₂)in/43 (43: 44: 44: 44)cm, ending with a WS row.

Shape top

Keeping patt correct, bind off 3 (4: 4: 5: 5) sts at beg of next 2 rows. *63 (63: 65: 65: 67) sts.*

Dec 1 st at each end of next 3 rows, then on foll 2 alt rows, then on every foll 4th row until 43 (43: 45: 45: 47) sts rem.

Work 1 row, ending with a WS row.

Dec 1 st at each end of next and every foll alt row to 37 sts, then on foll 5 rows, ending with a WS row.

Bind off rem 27 sts.

FINISHING

PRESS as described on the information page 138. Join both shoulder seams using back stitch, or mattress stitch if preferred.

Collar

Cast on 73 (77: 77: 85: 85) sts using size 10 (6mm) needles.

Work in patt as given for back for 12 rows, ending with a RS row.

Row 13 (dec) (WS): K1, P1, K1, P3tog, patt to last 6 sts, P3tog tbl, K1, P1, K1.

Work 3 rows.

Rep last 4 rows once more, then row 13 again. *61 (65: 65: 73: 73) sts.*

Work 1 row, ending with a RS row.

Place markers at both ends of last row.

Bind off 5 (6: 6: 7: 7) sts at beg of next 2 rows, then 8 (8: 8: 9: 9) sts at beg of foll 4 rows.

Bind off rem 19 (21: 21: 23: 23) sts.

Matching markers, sew shaped bound-off edge of collar to neck edge, then sew shaped row-end edges of collar to neck bound-off sts.

See information page 138 for finishing instructions, setting in sleeves using the set-in method.

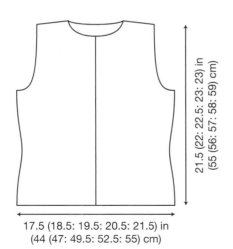

17.5 (18.5: 19.5: 20.5: 21.5) in
(44 (47: 49.5: 52.5: 55) cm)

21.5 (22: 22.5: 23: 23) in
(55 (56: 57: 58: 59) cm)

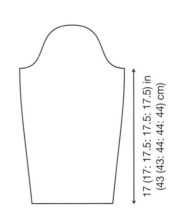

17 (17: 17.5: 17.5: 17.5) in
(43 (43: 44: 44: 44) cm)

Spangle

Two versions of a glamorous evening top, one with a boat neck and keyhole back and the other with a pretty polo neck. Both are knitted in soft, luxurious *Kidsilk Haze* to give them a dressy look and the polo neck version has optional beading for a further touch of glamour. Without the beads, the keyhole top makes a very simple knitting project.

YARN AND SIZES

	XS	S	M	L	XL	
To fit bust	32	34	36	38	40	in
	81	86	91	97	102	cm

Lightweight (CYCA Fine) yarn
Rowan *Kidsilk Haze* (70% super kid mohair; 30% silk; 229yd/25g)
Polo neck vest in Mud 652

3	3	3	3	4	balls

Keyhole back vest in Hurricane 632

2	3	3	3	3	balls

(Polo neck vest originally photographed in Toffee 598; keyhole back vest in Lord 593)

NEEDLES
1 pair size 2 (3mm) needles
1 pair size 3 (3.25mm) needles

Polo neck vest only: size 2 (3mm) circular needle

EXTRAS
Beads (optional) **polo neck vest only:** approx 750 beads
1 button for keyhole back vest

GAUGE
25 sts and 34 rows to 4in/10cm measured over stockinette stitch using size 3 (3.25mm) needles *or size necessary to obtain correct gauge*.

Polo neck vest
Beading note: Beads are optional. If using beads, thread them onto yarn before beginning, threading approx 250 beads onto first ball. Place beads within knitting as foll: bring yarn to front (RS) of work and slip next st purlwise, slide bead along yarn so that it sits in front of st just slipped, then take yarn to back (WS) of work.

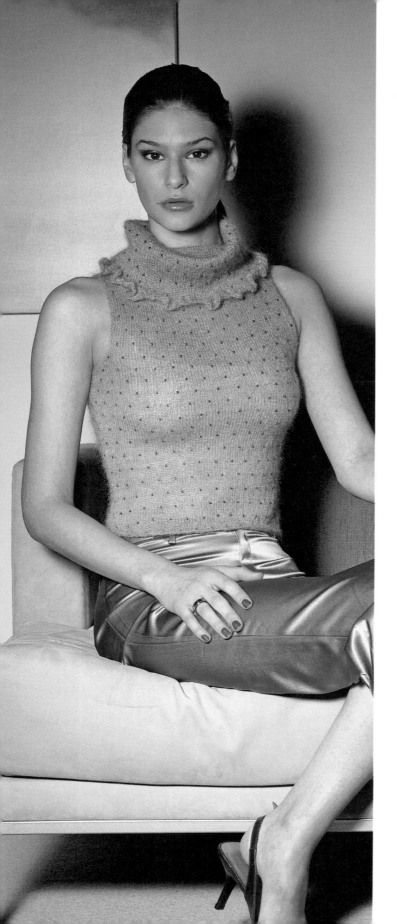

Polo neck vest

BACK

Cast on 95 (101: 107: 113: 119) sts using size 2 (3mm) needles.

Beg with a K row, work in St st for 4 rows.

Row 5 (RS): K5 (2: 5: 2: 5), *place bead (see beading note), K5, rep from * to last 6 (3: 6: 3: 6), place bead, K5 (2: 5: 2: 5).

Beg with a P row, work 3 rows in St st.

Change to size 3 (3.25mm) needles.

Work in St st for a further 4 rows, shaping side seams by dec 1 st at each end of 3rd of these rows. *93 (99: 105: 111: 117) sts.*

Row 13 (RS): K1 (4: 1: 4: 1), *place bead (see beading note), K5, rep from * to last 2 (5: 2: 5: 2), place bead, K1 (4: 1: 4: 1).

Beg with a P row, work 3 rows in St st.

These 16 rows set bead patt and begin side seam shaping.

Cont in patt, dec 1 st at each end of 3rd and foll 8th row. *89 (95: 101: 107: 113) sts.*

Work 13 rows, ending with a WS row.

Inc 1 st at each end of next and every foll 10th row until there are 101 (107: 113: 119: 125) sts, taking inc sts into patt.

Cont even until back measures 11$\frac{1}{2}$ (12: 12: 12$\frac{1}{4}$: 12$\frac{1}{4}$)in/29 (30: 30: 31: 31)cm, ending with a WS row.

Shape armholes

Keeping patt correct, bind off 4 (4: 5: 5: 6) sts at beg of next 2 rows, then 4 sts at beg of foll 2 rows. *85 (91: 95: 101: 105) sts.*

Dec 1 st at each end of next 3 (5: 5: 7: 7) rows, then on foll 4 (4: 5: 5: 6) alt rows. *71 (73: 75: 77: 79) sts.*

Cont even until armhole measures 8 (8: 8$\frac{1}{4}$: 8$\frac{1}{4}$: 8$\frac{3}{4}$)in/20 (20: 21: 21: 22)cm, ending with a WS row.

Shape shoulders and back neck

Bind off 4 (4: 4: 4: 5) sts at beg of next 2 rows. *63 (65: 67: 69: 69) sts.*

Next row (RS): Bind off 4 (4: 4: 4: 5) sts, patt until there are 8 (8: 9: 9: 8) sts on right needle and turn, leaving rem sts on a holder.
Work each side of neck separately.
Bind off 4 sts at beg of next row.
Bind off rem 4 (4: 5: 5: 4) sts.
With RS facing, rejoin yarn to rem sts, bind off center 39 (41: 41: 43: 43) sts, patt to end.
Work to match first side, reversing shapings.

FRONT

Work as given for back until 26 (26: 26: 28: 28) rows less have been worked before start of shoulder shaping, ending with a WS row.
Shape neck
Next row (RS): Patt 25 (25: 26: 27: 28) sts and turn, leaving rem sts on a holder.
Work each side of neck separately.
Bind off 5 sts at beg of next row.
20 (20: 21: 22: 23) sts.
Dec 1 st at neck edge on next 3 rows, then on foll 3 (3: 3: 4: 4) alt rows, then on every foll 4th row until 12 (12: 13: 13: 14) sts rem.
Work 7 rows, ending with a WS row.
Shape shoulder
Bind off 4 (4: 4: 4: 5) sts at beg of next and foll alt row.
Work 1 row.
Bind off rem 4 (4: 5: 5: 4) sts.
With RS facing, rejoin yarn to rem sts, bind off center 21 (23: 23: 23: 23) sts, patt to end.
Work to match first side, reversing shapings.

Keyhole back vest
FRONT

Working in St st throughout, work as given for back of polo neck vest until armhole measures 6¾ (6¾:7: 7: 7½)in/17 (17: 18: 18: 19)cm, ending with a WS row.

Shape neck
Next row (RS): K20 (20: 21: 21: 22) and turn, leaving rem sts on a holder.
Work each side of neck separately.
Bind off 6 sts at beg of next row.
14 (14: 15: 15: 16) sts.
Dec 1 st at neck edge on next 3 rows, then on foll 2 alt rows. *9 (9: 10: 10: 11) sts.*
Work 1 row, ending with a WS row.
Shape shoulder
Bind off 3 (3: 3: 3: 4) sts at beg of next and foll alt row.
Work 1 row.
Bind off rem 3 (3: 4: 4: 3) sts.
With RS facing, rejoin yarn to rem sts, bind off center 31 (33: 33: 35: 35) sts, K to end.
Work to match first side, reversing shapings.

BACK

Work as given for front until 6 rows fewer have been worked than on front to beg of armhole shaping, ending with a WS row.
Divide for back opening
Next row (RS): K49 (52: 55: 58: 61) and turn, leaving rem sts on a holder.
Work each side of neck separately.
Dec 1 st at back opening edge of next 4 rows.
45 (48: 51: 54: 57) sts.
Work 1 row, ending with a WS row.
Shape armhole
Bind off 4 (4: 5: 5: 6) sts at beg of next row, then 4 sts at beg of foll alt row **and at same time** dec 1 st at back opening edge on next and foll alt row.
35 (38: 40: 43: 45) sts.
Work 1 row.
Dec 1 st at armhole edge of next 3 (5: 5: 7: 7) rows, then on foll 2 (2: 3: 3: 4) alt rows.
30 (31: 32: 33: 34) sts.
Work 1 row.

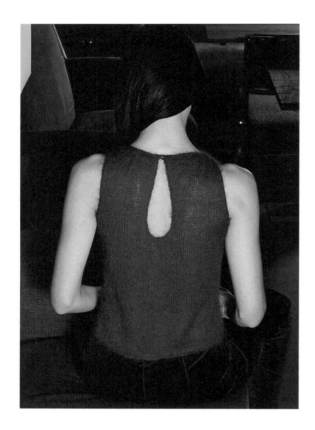

Dec 1 st at armhole edge of next and foll alt row **and at same time** inc 1 st at back opening edge of next row. *29 (30: 31: 32: 33) sts.*

Inc 1 st at back opening edge on every foll 10th row from previous inc until there are 31 (32: 33: 34: 35) sts, then on every foll 8th row until there are 34 (35: 36: 37: 38) sts.

Cont even until 3 rows fewer have been worked than on front to start of shoulder shaping, ending with a RS row.

Shape neck
Bind off 21 (22: 22: 23: 23) sts at beg of next row. *13 (13: 14: 14: 15) sts.*

Dec 1 st at neck edge on next 2 rows. *11 (11: 12: 12: 13) sts.*

Shape shoulder
Bind off 3 (3: 3: 3: 4) sts at beg and dec 1 st at end of next row.

Work 1 row.

Rep last 2 rows once more.

Bind off rem 3 (3: 4: 4: 3) sts.

With RS facing, rejoin yarn to rem sts, bind off 3 sts, K to end.

Work to match first side, reversing shapings.

FINISHING
PRESS all pieces as described on the information page 138.

Polo neck vest
Join right shoulder seam using back stitch, or mattress stitch if preferred.

Collar
With RS facing and size 2 (3mm) needles, pick up and knit 33 (33: 33: 35: 35) sts down left side of neck, 21 (23: 23: 23: 23) sts from front, 33 (33: 33: 35: 35) sts up right side of neck, then 46 (50: 50: 52: 52) sts from back. *133 (139: 139: 145: 145) sts.*

Beg with a K row, work in St st for 26 rows.

Break yarn, thread beads onto yarn and then rejoin yarn.

Next row (RS): K2, *place bead, K5, rep from * to last 5 sts, place bead, K4.

Work in St st for a further 7 rows.

Next row: *K5, place bead, rep from * to last st, K1.

Work in St st for a further 7 rows.

Last 16 rows form bead patt.

Cont in patt until collar measures 4in/10cm.

Change to size 3 (3.25mm) needles and cont in patt until collar measures 10in/25cm, ending with a WS row.

Work edging
Change to size 2 (3mm) circular needle.

Work in St st for a further 2 rows.

Next row (RS): *K1, M1, rep from * to last st, K1.

265 (277: 277: 289: 289) sts.
Purl 1 row
Next row: *K1, M1, rep from * to last st, P1.
529 (553: 553: 577: 577) sts.
Purl 1 row
Bind off knitwise.
Join left shoulder and collar seam using back stitch, or mattress stitch if preferred, reversing seam for turn-back.

Keyhole back vest

Back opening border

With RS facing and size 2 (3mm) needles, pick up and knit 58 (60: 60: 62: 62) sts down right side of back opening, then 58 (60: 60: 62: 62) sts up left side of back opening. *116 (120: 120: 124: 124) sts.*
Bind off knitwise.
Join both shoulder seams using back stitch, or mattress stitch if preferred.

Neckband

With RS facing and size 2 (3mm) needles, pick up and knit 29 (30: 30: 31: 31) sts up left side of back neck, 19 sts down left side of front neck, 31 (33: 33: 35: 35) sts from front, 19 sts up right side of front neck, then 29 (30: 30: 31: 31) sts down right side of back neck. *127 (131: 131: 135: 135) sts.*
Bind off knitwise.

Make button loop and attach button to fasten back opening at neck edge.

Both vests

Armhole borders (both alike)

With RS facing and size 2 (3mm) needles, pick up and knit 120 (120: 127: 127: 134) sts evenly around armhole edge.
Bind off knitwise.
See information page 138 for finishing instructions.

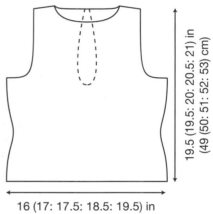

16 (17: 17.5: 18.5: 19.5) in
(40.5 (43: 45: 47.5: 50) cm)

19.5 (19.5: 20: 20.5: 21) in
(49 (50: 51: 52: 53) cm)

Alex

This great, classic turtleneck sweater has been given a contemporary feel with a cropped length and three-quarter sleeves. Any one of the new bright shades in Rowan *Wool Cotton*, which is a yarn that knits up with a defined finish, would look great as a substitute for the orange. It would make a good project for a relatively inexperienced knitter. However, because it is knitted in stockinette stitch, you need to keep a good even gauge throughout. Do not be tempted to stop knitting in the middle of a row, as the resulting stitches will stretch and show up. Always stop knitting at the end of a row!

YARN AND SIZES

	XS	S	M	L	XL	
To fit bust	32	34	36	38	40	in
	81	86	91	97	102	cm

DK (CYCA Light) yarn
Rowan *Wool Cotton* (50% merino wool, 50% cotton; 123yd/50g) in Elf 946

	7	8	8	8	9	balls

(Originally photographed in Mango 950)

NEEDLES
1 pair size 3 (3.25mm) needles
1 pair size 6 (4mm) needles

GAUGE
22 sts and 30 rows to 4in/10cm measured over stockinette stitch using size 6 (4mm) needles *or size necessary to obtain correct gauge.*

BACK

Cast on 73 (79: 85: 91: 97) sts using size 3 (3.25mm) needles.

Row 1 (RS): K0 (1: 0: 2: 0), P0 (2: 1: 2: 2), *K3, P2, rep from * to last 3 (1: 4: 2: 0) sts, K3 (1: 3: 2: 0), P0 (0: 1: 0: 0).

Row 2: P0 (1: 0: 2: 0), K0 (2: 1: 2: 2), *P3, K2, rep from * to last 3 (1: 4: 2: 0) sts, P3 (1: 3: 2: 0), K0 (0: 1: 0: 0).

These 2 rows form rib.

Work in rib for a further 16 rows, ending with a WS row.

Change to size 6 (4mm) needles.

Beg with a K row, work in St st as foll:

Work 2 rows, ending with a WS row.

Next row (RS): K2, M1, K to last 2 sts, M1, K2.

Working all increases as set by last row, cont in St st, shaping sides by inc 1 st at each end of 5th and every foll 6th row to 83 (89: 95: 101: 107) sts, then on every foll 8th row until there are 89 (95: 101: 107: 113) sts.

Cont even until back measures 11in/28cm, ending with a WS row.

Shape raglan armholes

Bind off 6 sts at beg of next 2 rows.
77 (83: 89: 95: 101) sts.

Extra small size only

Next row (RS): P2, K2tog, K to last 4 sts, K2tog tbl, P2. *75 sts.*

Next row: K2, P to last 2 sts, K2.

Next row: P2, K to last 2 sts, P2.

Next row: K2, P to last 2 sts, K2.

Medium, large, and extra large sizes only

Next row (RS): P2, K3tog, K to last 5 sts, K3tog tbl, P2.

Next row: K2, P to last 2 sts, K2.

Rep last 2 rows - (-: 1: 2: 4) times more.
- (-: 81: 83: 81) sts.

All sizes

Next row (RS): P2, K2tog, K to last 4 sts, K2tog tbl,

P2.

Next row: K2, P to last 2 sts, K2.

Rep last 2 rows 23 (26: 25: 25: 24) times more, ending with a WS row.

Bind off rem 27 (29: 29: 31: 31) sts.

FRONT

Work as given for back until 41 (43: 43: 47: 47) sts rem in raglan shaping.

Work 1 row, ending with a WS row.

Shape neck

Next row (RS): P2, K2tog, K8 (8: 8: 10: 10) and turn, leaving rem sts on a holder. *11 (11: 11: 13: 13) sts.*

Work each side of neck separately.

Working all raglan decreases as set, dec 1 st at neck edge of next 2 rows, then on foll 2 (2: 2: 3: 3) alt rows and at same time dec 1 st at raglan edge of 2nd and every foll alt row. *4 sts.*

Next row (WS): P2, K2.

Next row: P1, P3tog.

Next row: K2.

Next row: P2tog and fasten off.

With RS facing, rejoin yarn to rem sts, bind off center 17 (19: 19: 19: 19) sts, K to last 4 sts, K2tog tbl, P2. *11 (11: 11: 13: 13) sts.*

Complete to match first side, reversing shapings.

SLEEVES

Cast on 55 (55: 57: 59: 59) sts using size 3 (3.25mm) needles.

Row 1 (RS): K0 (0: 0: 1: 1), P1 (1: 2: 2: 2), *K3, P2, rep from * to last 4 (4: 0: 1: 1) sts, K3 (3: 0: 1: 1), P1 (1: 0: 0: 0).

Row 2: P0 (0: 0: 1: 1), K1 (1: 2: 2: 2), *P3, K2, rep from * to last 4 (4: 0: 1: 1) sts, P3 (3: 0: 1: 1), K1 (1: 0: 0: 0).

These 2 rows form rib.

Work in rib for a further 16 rows, inc 1 st at each end of 9th of these rows and ending with a WS row. *57 (57: 59: 61: 61) sts.*

Change to size 6 (4mm) needles.

Beg with a K row and working all increases as given for side seam increases, work in St st, shaping sides by inc 1 st at each end of 3rd and every foll 6th row until there are 81 (83: 85: 87: 89) sts.

Cont even until sleeve measures 13³/₄ (13³/₄: 14: 14: 14)in/35 (35: 36: 36: 36)cm, ending with a WS row.

Shape raglan

Bind off 6 sts at beg of next 2 rows.

69 (71: 73: 75: 77) sts.

Working all raglan decreases as given for back and front, dec 1 st at each end of next and every foll alt row until 21 sts rem.

Work 1 row, ending with a WS row.

Left sleeve only

Dec 1 st at each end of next row. *19 sts.*

Bind off 5 sts at beg of next row. *14 sts.*

Dec 1 st at beg of next row. *13 sts.*

Bind off 6 sts at beg of next row. *7 sts.*

Right sleeve only

Bind off 6 sts at beg and dec 1 st at end of next row. *14 sts.*

Work 1 row. Rep last 2 rows once more. *7 sts.*

Both sleeves

Bind off rem 7 sts.

FINISHING

PRESS as described on the information page 138. Join both front and right back raglan seams using back stitch, or mattress stitch if preferred.

Neckband

With RS facing and using size 3 (3.25mm) needles, pick up and knit 19 sts from left sleeve, 10 (11: 11: 12: 12) sts down left side of neck, 17 (19: 19: 19: 19) sts from front, 10 (11: 11: 12: 12) sts up right side of neck, 19 sts from right sleeve, then 27 (28: 28: 31: 31) sts from back. *102 (107: 107: 112: 112) sts.*

Row 1 (WS): K2, *P3, K2, rep from * to end.

Row 2: P2, *K3, P2, rep from * to end.

Rep these 2 rows until neckband measures 2¹/₂in/6cm.

Bind off in rib.

See information page 138 for finishing instructions.

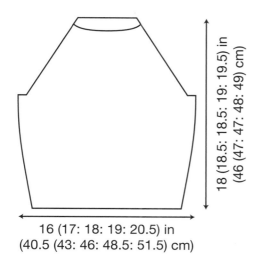

16 (17: 18: 19: 20.5) in
(40.5 (43: 46: 48.5: 51.5) cm)

18 (18.5: 18.5: 19: 19.5) in
(46 (47: 47: 48: 49) cm)

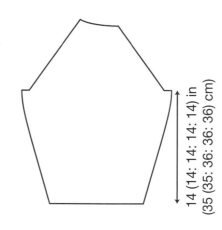

14 (14: 14: 14: 14) in
(35 (35: 36: 36: 36) cm)

Jess

This great summery cardigan is knitted in *Denim* yarn, which is perennially popular. The collar can be worn up, as shown, or dropped back to form a more traditional flat rever. Truly great shaping detail makes this longer length cardigan a singularly elegant shape and the seed stitch button band adds a crisp finish. *Denim* does shrink the first time it is washed, but allowance has been made for this in the pattern sizing. However, it is a yarn that becomes more beautiful as it is washed.

YARN AND SIZES

	XS	S	M	L	XL	
To fit bust	32	34	36	38	40	in
	81	86	91	97	102	cm

DK (CYCA Light) yarn
Rowan *Denim* (100% cotton; 102yd/50g)
in Nashville 225

	15	16	17	18	18	balls

NEEDLES
1 pair size 3 (3.25mm) needles
1 pair size 5 (3.75mm) needles
1 pair size 6 (4mm) needles

EXTRAS
Buttons: 11 x Rowan 75319

GAUGE
Before washing: 20 sts and 28 rows to 4in/10cm measured over stockinette stitch using size 6 (4mm) needles *or size necessary to obtain correct gauge.*

Gauge note: *Denim* will shrink in length when washed for the first time. Allowances have been made in the pattern for shrinkage (see size diagram for after washing measurements).

BACK

Cast on 91 (95: 101: 105: 111) sts using size 5 (3.75mm) needles.

Row 1 (RS): K2 (4: 3: 5: 4), [P2, K2] 3 (3: 4: 4: 5) times, *P3, K2, rep from * to last 12 (14: 17: 19: 22) sts, [P2, K2] 3 (3: 4: 4: 5) times, K0 (2: 1: 3: 2).

Row 2: P2 (4: 3: 5: 4), [K2, P2] 3 (3: 4: 4: 5) times, *K3, P2, rep from * to last 12 (14: 17: 19: 22) sts, [K2, P2] 3 (3: 4: 4: 5) times, P0 (2: 1: 3: 2).

Rep last 2 rows 3 times more.

Change to size 6 (4mm) needles and work as foll:

Row 1 (RS): Rib 14 (16: 19: 21: 24), P to last 14 (16: 19: 21: 24) sts, rib to end.

Row 2: Rib 14 (16: 19: 21: 24), K to last 14 (16: 21: 24) sts, rib to end.

These 2 rows set the sts—center sts in rev St st with edge sts still in rib.

Keeping sts correct as set, work a further 6 rows, ending with a WS row.

Row 9 (RS) (dec): Rib 14 (16: 19: 21: 24), P1, P2tog, P to last 17 (19: 22: 24: 27) sts, P2tog tbl, P1, rib to end. *89 (93: 99: 103: 109) sts.*

Working all decreases as set by last row, dec 1 st at each end of every foll 6th row until 73 (77: 83: 87: 93) sts rem.

Work 9 rows, ending with a WS row.

Next row (RS) (inc): Rib 14 (16: 19: 21: 24), P1, M1, P to last 15 (17: 20: 22: 25) sts, M1, P1, rib to end.

Working all increases as set by last row, inc 1 st at each end of every foll 6th row until there are 91 (95: 101: 105: 111) sts.

Work 2 rows, ending with a RS row.

Next row (WS): Rib 13 (15: 18: 20: 23), K to last 13 (15: 18: 20: 23) sts, rib to end.

Next row: Rib 12 (14: 17: 19: 22), P to last 12 (14: 17: 19: 22) sts, rib to end.

Next row: Rib 10 (12: 15: 17: 20), K to last 10 (12: 15: 17: 20) sts, rib to end.

Next row: Rib 9 (11: 14: 16: 19), P to last 9 (11: 14: 16: 19) sts, rib to end.

Next row: Rib 8 (10: 13: 15: 18), K to last 8 (10: 13: 15: 18) sts, rib to end.

Next row: Rib 6 (8: 11: 13: 16), P to last 6 (8: 11: 13: 16) sts, rib to end.

Next row: Rib 5 (7: 10: 12: 15), K to last 5 (7: 10: 12: 15) sts, rib to end.

Next row: Rib 4 (6: 9: 11: 14), P to last 4 (6: 9: 11: 14) sts, rib to end.

Next row: Rib 2 (4: 7: 9: 12), K to last 2 (4: 7: 9: 12) sts, rib to end.

Next row: Rib 1 (3: 6: 8: 11), P to last 1 (3: 6: 8: 11) sts, rib to end.

Next row: Rib 0 (2: 5: 7: 10), K to last 0 (2: 5: 7: 10) sts, rib 0 (2: 5: 7: 10).

Work should measure approx 19in/48.5cm.

Shape raglan armholes

Now working all sts in rev St st, bind off 5 sts at beg of next 2 rows. *81 (85: 91: 95: 101) sts.*

Dec 1 st at each end of next 1 (1: 5: 5: 9) rows, then on every foll alt row until 17 (19: 19: 21: 21) sts rem.

Work 1 row, ending with a WS row.

Bind off rem 17 (19: 19: 21: 21) sts.

LEFT FRONT

Cast on 45 (47: 50: 52: 55) sts using size 5 (3.75mm) needles.

Row 1 (RS): K2 (4: 3: 5: 4), [P2, K2] 3 (3: 4: 4: 5) times, *P3, K2, rep from * to last st, P1.

Row 2: K1, P2, *K3, P2, rep from * to last 12 (14: 17: 19: 22) sts, [K2, P2] 3 (3: 4: 4: 5) times, P0 (2: 1: 3: 2).

Rep last 2 rows 3 times more.

Change to size 6 (4mm) needles and work as foll:

Row 1 (RS): Rib 14 (16: 19: 21: 24), P to end.

Row 2: K to last 14 (16: 19: 21: 24) sts, rib to end.

These 2 rows set the sts—center front sts in rev St st with edge sts still in rib.

Keeping sts correct as set, work 6 rows, ending

120

with a WS row.

Row 9 (RS) (dec): Rib 14 (16: 19: 21: 24), P1, P2tog, P to end.

Working all decreases as set by last row, dec 1 st at beg of every foll 6th row until 36 (38: 41: 43: 46) sts rem.

Work 9 rows, ending with a WS row.

Next row (RS) (inc): Rib 14 (16: 19: 21: 24), P1, M1, P to end.

Working all increases as set by last row, inc 1 st at beg of every foll 6th row until there are 45 (47: 50: 52: 55) sts.

Work 2 rows, ending with a RS row.

Next row (WS): K to last 13 (15: 18: 20: 23) sts, rib to end.

Next row: Rib 12 (14: 17: 19: 22), P to end.

Next row: K to last 10 (12: 15: 17: 20) sts, rib to end.

Next row: Rib 9 (11: 14: 16: 19), P to end.

Next row: K to last 8 (10: 13: 15: 18) sts, rib to end.

Next row: Rib 6 (8: 11: 13: 16), P to end.

Next row: K to last 5 (7: 10: 12: 15) sts, rib to end.

Next row: Rib 4 (6: 9: 11: 14), P to end.

Next row: K to last 2 (4: 7: 9: 12) sts, rib to end.

Next row: Rib 1 (3: 6: 8: 11), P to end.

Next row: K to last 0 (2: 5: 7: 10) sts, rib 0 (2: 5: 7: 10).

Shape raglan armhole

Now working all sts in rev St st, bind off 5 sts at beg of next row. *40 (42: 45: 47: 50) sts.*

Work 1 row.

Dec 1 st at raglan edge of next 1 (1: 5: 5: 9) rows, then on every foll alt row until 16 (17: 17: 19: 19) sts rem, ending with a RS row.

Shape neck

Bind off 4 (5: 5: 5: 5) sts at beg of next row. *12 (12: 12: 14: 14) sts.*

Dec 1 st at neck edge of next 3 rows, then on foll 1 (1: 1: 2: 2) alt rows, then on foll 4th row **and at**

same time dec 1 st at raglan edge on next and every foll alt row. *2 sts.*

Work 1 row, ending with a WS row.

P2tog and fasten off.

RIGHT FRONT

Cast on 45 (47: 50: 52: 55) sts using size 5 (3.75mm) needles.

Row 1 (RS): P1, K2, *P3, K2, rep from * to last 12 (14: 17: 19: 22) sts, [P2, K2] 3 (3: 4: 4: 5) times, K0 (2: 1: 3: 2).

Row 2: P2 (4: 3: 5: 4), [K2, P2] 3 (3: 4: 4: 5) times, *K3, P2, rep from * to last st, K1.

Rep last 2 rows 3 times more.

Change to size 6 (4mm) needles and work as foll:

Row 1 (RS): P to last 14 (16: 19: 21: 24) sts, rib to end.

Row 2: Rib 14 (16: 19: 21: 24), K to end.

These 2 rows set the sts—center front sts in rev St st with edge sts still in rib.

Keeping sts correct as set, work 6 rows, ending with a WS row.

Row 9 (RS) (dec): P to last 17 (19: 22: 24: 27) sts, P2tog tbl, P1, rib 14 (16: 19: 21: 24).

Complete to match left front, reversing shapings.

SLEEVES

Cast on 45 (45: 47: 49: 49) sts using size 5 (3.75mm) needles.

Row 1 (RS): K4 (4: 5: 6: 6), [P2, K2] 3 times, (P3, K2] twice, P3, [K2, P2] 3 times, K4 (4: 5: 6: 6).

Row 2: P4 (4: 5: 6: 6), [K2, P2] 3 times, [K3, P2] twice, K3, [P2, K2] 3 times, P4 (4: 5: 6: 6).

Rep last 2 rows 3 times more.

Change to size 6 (4mm) needles and work as foll:

Row 1 (RS): Rib 16 (16: 17: 18: 18), P to last 16 (16: 17: 18: 18) sts, rib to end.

Row 2: Rib 16 (16: 17: 18: 18), K to last 16 (16: 17: 18: 18) sts, rib to end.

These 2 rows set the sts—center sts in rev St st

with edge sts still in rib.

Keeping sts correct as set, work 2 rows, ending with a WS row.

Row 5 (RS) (inc): Rib 16 (16: 17: 18: 18), P1, M1, P to last 17 (17: 18: 19: 19) sts, M1, P1, rib to end.

Working all increases as set by last row, inc 1 st at each end of every foll 10th row to 51 (63: 61: 63: 75) sts, then on every foll 12th row until there are 69 (71: 73: 75: 77) sts.

Next row (WS): Rib 15 (15: 16: 17: 17), K to last 15 (15: 16: 17: 17) sts, rib to end.

Next row: Rib 14 (14: 15: 16: 16), P to last 14 (14: 15: 16: 16) sts, rib to end.

Next row: Rib 12 (12: 13: 14: 14), K to last 12 (12: 13: 14: 14) sts, rib to end.

Next row: Rib 11 (11: 12: 13: 13), P to last 11 (11: 12: 13: 13) sts, rib to end.

Next row: Rib 10 (10: 11: 12: 12), K to last 10 (10: 11: 12: 12) sts, rib to end.

Next row: Rib 8 (8: 9: 10: 10), P to last 8 (8: 9: 10: 10) sts, rib to end.

Next row: Rib 7 (7: 8: 9: 9), K to last 7 (7: 8: 9: 9) sts, rib to end.

Next row: Rib 6 (6: 7: 8: 8), P to last 6 (6: 7: 8: 8) sts, rib to end.

Next row: Rib 4 (4: 5: 6: 6), K to last 4 (4: 5: 6: 6) sts, rib to end.

Next row: Rib 3 (3: 4: 5: 5), P to last 3 (3: 4: 5: 5) sts, rib to end.

Next row: Rib 2 (2: 3: 4: 4), K to last 2 (2: 3: 4: 4) sts, rib to end.

Shape raglan

Keeping sts correct as set, bind off 5 sts at beg of next 2 rows. *59 (61: 63: 65: 67) sts.*

Dec 1 st at each end of next and every foll 4th row to 43 (45: 47: 49: 51) sts, then on every foll alt row until 15 sts rem.

Work 1 row, ending with a WS row.

Left sleeve only

Dec 1 st at each end of next row. *13 sts.*

Bind off 2 sts at beg of next row. *11 sts.*

Dec 1 st at beg of next row, then bind off 3 sts at beg of foll row. *7 sts.*

Rep last 2 rows once more. *3 sts.*

Right sleeve only

Bind off 3 sts at beg and dec 1 st at end of next row. *11 sts.*

Work 1 row.

Rep last 2 rows twice more. *3 sts.*

Both sleeves

Bind off rem 3 sts.

FINISHING

DO NOT PRESS.

Join raglan seams using back stitch, or mattress stitch if preferred.

Button band

Cast on 6 sts using size 3 (3.25mm) needles.

Row 1 (RS): [K1, P1] 3 times.

Row 2: [P1, K1] 3 times.

These 2 rows form seed st.

Cont in seed st until band, when slightly stretched, fits up left front opening edge to neck shaping, ending with a WS row.

Break yarn and leave sts on a holder.

Sl st band in place.

Mark positions for 10 buttons on this band—first button 8 rows up from cast-on edge, 4th button to come midway between last waist dec and first waist inc, 2nd and 3rd buttons evenly spaced between these 2, 10th button 3/8in/1cm down from neck edge, and 5th, 6th, 7th, 8th, and 9th buttons evenly spaced between 4th and 10th buttons.

Buttonhole band

Work as for button band, with the addition of 10 buttonholes to correspond with positions marked on button band for buttons, worked as foll:

Buttonhole row (RS): K1, P1, P2tog, yo, K1, P1.

When band is complete, ending with a WS row, do

NOT break off yarn.

Sl st band in place.

Collar

With RS facing and using size 3 (3.25mm)
needles, seed st across 6 sts of buttonhole band,
pick up and knit 18 (18: 18: 20: 20) sts up right
side of neck, 10 sts from right sleeve, 18 (18: 18:
22: 22) sts from back, 10 sts from left sleeve, and
18 (18: 18: 20: 20) sts down left side of neck, then
seed st across 6 sts of button band.
86 (86: 86: 94: 94) sts.

Row 1 (WS): Seed st 6 sts, *P2, K2, rep from * to
last 8 sts, P2, seed st 6 sts.

Row 2: Seed st 6 sts, *K2, P2, rep from * to last 8
sts, K2, seed st 6 sts.

Last 2 rows set the sts.

Working an 11th buttonhole in same way as
for previous buttonholes and positioning this
buttonhole same distance above 10th as between
9th and 10th buttonholes, cont as set until collar
measures 3in/8cm from pick-up row, ending with
a WS row.

Next row (RS): Bind off 6 sts, patt to last 6 sts,
bind off rem 6 sts. *74 (74: 74: 82: 82) sts.*

Rejoin yarn with WS facing and, beg with a P row,
work in St st for 3in/8cm.

Bind off.

Machine wash all pieces before completing
sewing together.

Fold St st section of collar to inside and sl st in
place.

See information page 138 for finishing
instructions.

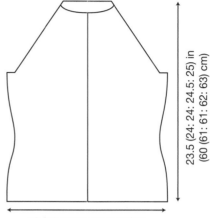

23.5 (24: 24: 24.5: 25) in
(60 (61: 61: 62: 63) cm)

18 (18.5: 20: 20.5: 22) in
(45.5 (47.5: 50.5: 52.5: 55.5) cm)

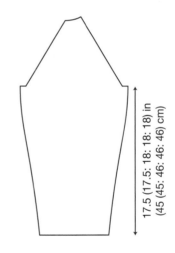

17.5 (17.5: 18: 18: 18) in
(45 (45: 46: 46: 46) cm)

Agnes

This design is a peach! It makes the perfect little fitted jacket, with its gently rolling seed-stitch collar and deep seed-stitch peplum. It is a really versatile design, looking just as good, as here, with a full skirt, or over a pair of cropped pants. The regularly spaced tiny French knots in a contrasting color add interest to the design (and more fun for the knitter!). *Cotton Glace* is a great yarn, with a slight sheen to it. It is perfect for this style of garment, which needs a crisp finish but with a smooth texture.

YARN AND SIZES

	XS	S	M	L	XL	
To fit bust	32	34	36	38	40	in
	81	86	91	97	102	cm

DK (CYCA Light) yarn
Rowan *Cotton Glace* (100% cotton; 126yd/50g)

	XS	S	M	L	XL	
A Whey 834	10	11	12	12	13	balls
B Umber 838	1	1	1	1	1	balls

(Originally photographed in Oyster 730 and Mocha Choc 816)

NEEDLES
1 pair size 2 (3mm) needles
1 pair size 3 (3.25mm) needles

EXTRAS
Buttons: 8 x Rowan 75320

GAUGE
23 sts and 39 rows to 4in/10cm measured over seed stitch, 23 sts and 32 rows to 4in/10cm measured over stockinette stitch using size 3 (3.25mm) needles *or size necessary to obtain correct gauge.*

BACK

Lower section

Cast on 99 (105: 111: 117: 123) sts using size 2 (3mm) needles and yarn A.

Row 1 (RS): K1, *P1, K1, rep from * to end.

Row 2: As row 1.

These 2 rows form seed st.

Work in seed st for a further 4 rows, ending with a WS row.

Change to size 3 (3.25mm) needles.

Work a further 14 rows, ending with a WS row.

Place markers on 26th (28th: 30th: 32nd: 34th) st in from both ends of last row.

Next row (RS): Work 2 tog, seed st to within 1 st of first marker, work 3 tog (marked st is center st of this group), seed st to within 1 st of 2nd marker, work 3 tog (marked st is center st of this group), seed st to last 2 sts, work 2 tog.

Work 15 rows.

Rep last 16 rows once more, then first of these rows (the dec row) again. *81 (87: 93: 99: 105) sts.*

Work a further 9 rows, ending with a WS row.

Bind off in seed st.

Upper section

With WS facing (so that ridge is formed on RS of work), using size 3 (3.25mm) needles and yarn A, pick up and knit 81 (87: 93: 99: 105) sts across bound-off edge of lower section.

Beg with a K row, work in St st for 8 rows, ending with a WS row.

Cont in patt as foll:

Row 1 (RS): K2, M1, K6 (1: 4: 7: 2), *P1, K7, rep from * to last 9 (4: 7: 10: 5) sts, P1, K6 (1: 4: 7: 2), M1, K2.

Working all side seam increases as set by last row and beg with a P row, work in St st for 9 rows, inc 1 st at each end of 6th of these rows. *85 (91: 97: 103: 109) sts.*

Row 11 (RS): K6 (9: 4: 7: 2), *P1, K7, rep from * to last 7 (10: 5: 8: 3) sts, P1, K6 (9: 4: 7: 2).

Beg with a P row, work in St st for 9 rows, inc 1 st at each end of 2nd and foll 6th row. *89 (95: 101: 107: 113) sts.*

Last 20 rows form patt and start side seam shaping.

Cont in patt, shaping side seams by inc 1 st at each end of 5th and every foll 6th row to 95 (101: 107: 113: 119) sts, then on every foll 4th row until there are 99 (105: 111: 117: 123) sts, taking inc sts into patt.

Cont even until back measures 13¾ (14: 14: 14½: 14½)in/35 (36: 36: 37: 37)cm **from cast-on edge of lower section**, ending with a WS row.

Shape armholes

Keeping patt correct, bind off 3 (4: 4: 5: 5) sts at beg of next 2 rows. *93 (97: 103: 107: 113) sts.*

Dec 1 st at each end of next 5 (5: 7: 7: 9) rows, then on foll 2 (3: 3: 4: 4) alt rows, then on foll 4th row. *77 (79: 81: 83: 85) sts.*

Cont even until armhole measures 8 (8: 8¼: 8¼: 8¾)in/20 (20: 21: 21: 22)cm, ending with a WS row.

Shape shoulders and back neck

Bind off 8 sts at beg of next 2 rows. *61 (63: 65: 67: 69) sts.*

Next row (RS): Bind off 8 sts, patt until there are 11 (11: 12: 12: 13) sts on right needle and turn, leaving rem sts on a holder.

Work each side of neck separately.

Bind off 4 sts at beg of next row.

Bind off rem 7 (7: 8: 8: 9) sts.

With RS facing, rejoin yarn to rem sts, bind off center 23 (25: 25: 27: 27) sts, patt to end.

Complete to match first side, reversing shapings.

LEFT FRONT

Lower section

Cast on 53 (56: 59: 62: 65) sts using size 2 (3mm) needles and yarn A.

Row 1 (RS): *K1, P1, rep from * to last 1 (0: 1: 0:

1) st, K1 (0: 1: 0: 1).

Row 2: K1 (0: 1: 0: 1), *P1, K1, rep from * to end.
These 2 rows form seed st.

Work in seed st for a further 4 rows, ending with a WS row.

Change to size 3 (3.25mm) needles.

Work a further 14 rows, ending with a WS row.

Place marker on 26th (28th: 30th: 32nd: 34th) st in from end of last row.

Next row (RS): Work 2 tog, seed st to within 1 st of marker, work 3 tog (marked st is center st of this group), seed st to end.

Work 15 rows.

Rep last 16 rows once more, then first of these rows (the dec row) again. *44 (47: 50: 53: 56) sts.*

Work a further 9 rows, ending with a WS row.

Next row (RS): Bind off first 39 (42: 45: 48: 51) sts, seed st to end.

Do NOT break yarn.

Upper section

Using size 3 (3.25mm) needles and yarn A, seed st 5 sts on needle, then with WS facing (so that ridge is formed on RS of work), pick up and knit 39 (42: 45: 48: 51) sts across bound-off edge of lower section. *44 (47: 50: 53: 56) sts.*

Next row (RS): K to last 5 sts, seed st 5 sts.

Next row: Seed st 5 sts, P to end.

These 2 rows set the sts—front opening edge 5 sts still in seed st with all other sts in St st.

Work a further 6 rows as set, ending with a WS row.

Cont in patt as foll:

Row 1 (RS): K2, M1, K6 (1: 4: 7: 2), *P1, K7, rep from * to last 12 sts, P1, K6, seed st 5 sts.

Working all side seam increases as set by last row, keeping seed st border correct and working all other sts in St st, beg with a P row, work 9 rows, inc 1 st at beg of 6th of these rows. *46 (49: 52: 55: 58) sts.*

Row 11 (RS): K6 (9: 4: 7: 2), *P1, K7, rep from * to

Special tip

FRENCH KNOT

These little jewel-like stitches are created by winding the yarn around the needle in the course of making the stitch, so that each stitch resembles a small bead. They are useful for creating textural effects. The number of times you wrap the thread around the needle increases the size of the knot. Practice will help to create neat, even knots.

last 8 sts, P1, K2, seed st 5 sts.

Work 9 rows, inc 1 st at beg of 2nd and foll 6th row. *48 (51: 54: 57: 60) sts.*

Last 20 rows form patt and start side seam shaping.

Cont in patt, shaping side seam by inc 1 st at beg of 5th and every foll 6th row to 51 (54: 57: 60: 63) sts, then on every foll 4th row until there are 53 (56: 59: 62: 65) sts, taking inc sts into patt.

Cont even until left front matches back to beg of armhole shaping, ending with a WS row.

Shape armhole

Keeping patt correct, bind off 3 (4: 4: 5: 5) sts at beg of next row. *50 (52: 55: 57: 60) sts.*

Work 1 row.

Dec 1 st at armhole edge of next 5 (5: 7: 7: 9) rows, then on foll 2 (3: 3: 4: 4) alt rows, then on foll 4th row. *42 (43: 44: 45: 46) sts.*

Cont even until 22 (22: 22: 24: 24) rows fewer have been worked to start of shoulder shaping, ending with a WS row.

Shape lapel

Next row (RS): Patt to last 5 sts, seed st 5 sts.

Next row: Seed st 6 sts, P to end.

Next row: Patt to last 7 sts, seed st 7 sts.

Next row: Seed st 8 sts, P to end.

Work 8 (9: 9: 10: 10) rows, working one extra st in seed on every row as set by last 4 rows (16 (17: 17: 18: 18) sts now in seed st).

Work a further 10 (9: 9: 10: 10) rows but now working one extra st in seed st on 3rd and every foll 3rd row, ending with a WS row (19 (20: 20: 21: 21) sts now in seed st).

Shape shoulder

Bind off 8 sts at beg of next and foll alt row, then 7 (7: 8: 8: 9) sts at beg of foll alt row.

Work 1 row, ending with a WS row.

Break yarn and leave rem 19 (20: 20: 21: 21) sts on a holder.

Mark positions for 7 buttons along opening edge of upper section, first to come in row 5, last to come 6 rows below lapel shaping, and rem 5 buttons evenly spaced between.

RIGHT FRONT
Lower section
Cast on 53 (56: 59: 62: 65) sts using size 2 (3mm) needles and yarn A.

Row 1 (RS): K1 (0: 1: 0: 1), *P1, K1, rep from * to end.

Row 2: *K1, P1, rep from * to last 1 (0: 1: 0: 1) st, K1 (0: 1: 0: 1).

These 2 rows form seed st.

Work in seed st for a further 4 rows, ending with a WS row.

Change to size 3 (3.25mm) needles.

Work a further 14 rows, ending with a WS row.

Place marker on 26th (28th: 30th: 32nd: 34th) st in from beg of last row.

Next row (RS): Seed st to within 1 st of marker, work 3 tog (marked st is center st of this group), seed st to last 2 sts, work 2 tog.

Work 15 rows.

Rep last 16 rows once more, then first of these rows (the dec row) again. *44 (47: 50: 53: 56) sts.*

Work a further 3 rows, ending with a WS row.

Next row (RS): Seed st 2 sts, work 2 tog, yo (to make first buttonhole), seed st to end.

Work a further 5 rows, ending with a WS row.

Next row (RS): Seed st 5 sts, bind off rem 39 (42: 45: 48: 51) sts.

Upper section
with WS facing (so that ridge is formed on RS of work), using size 3 (3.25mm) needles and yarn A, pick up and knit 39 (42: 45: 48: 51) sts across bound-off edge of lower section, then seed st rem 5 sts. *44 (47: 50: 53: 56) sts.*

Next row (RS): Seed st 5 sts, K to end.

Next row: P to last 5 sts, seed st 5 sts.

These 2 rows set the sts—front opening edge 5 sts still in seed st with all other sts in St st.

Work a further 2 rows as set, ending with a WS row.

Next row (RS): Seed st 2 sts, work 2 tog, yo (to make a buttonhole), patt to end.

Working a further 6 buttonholes in this way to correspond with positions marked for buttons on left front and noting that no further reference will be made to buttonholes, cont as foll:

Work a further 3 rows as set, ending with a WS row.

Cont in patt as foll:

Row 1 (RS): Seed st 5 sts, K6, *P1, K7, rep from * to last 9 (4: 7: 10: 5) sts, P1, K6 (1: 4: 7: 2), M1, K2.

Working all side seam increases as set by last row, keeping seed st border correct and working all other sts in St st, beg with a P row, work 9 rows, inc 1 st at end of 6th of these rows. *46 (49: 52: 55: 58) sts.*

Row 11 (RS): Seed st 5 sts, K2, *P1, K7, rep from * to last 7 (10: 5: 8: 3) sts, P1, K6 (9: 4: 7: 2).

Work 9 rows, inc 1 st at end of 2nd and foll 6th row. *48 (51: 54: 57: 60) sts.*

Last 20 rows form patt and start side seam shaping.

Cont in patt, shaping side seam by inc 1 st at end of 5th and every foll 6th row to 51 (54: 57: 60: 63) sts, then on every foll 4th row until there are 53 (56: 59: 62: 65) sts, taking inc sts into patt.

Cont even until right front matches back to beg of armhole shaping, ending with a RS row.

Shape armhole
Keeping patt correct, bind off 3 (4: 4: 5: 5) sts at beg of next row. *50 (52: 55: 57: 60) sts.*

Dec 1 st at armhole edge of next 5 (5: 7: 7: 9) rows, then on foll 2 (3: 3: 4: 4) alt rows, then on foll 4th row. *42 (43: 44: 45: 46) sts.*

Cont even until 22 (22: 22: 24: 24) rows fewer have been worked to start of shoulder shaping, ending with a WS row.

Shape lapel

Next row (RS): Seed st 5 sts, patt to end.
Next row: Patt to last 6 sts, seed st 6 sts.
Next row: Seed st 7 sts, patt to end.
Next row: Patt to last 8 sts, seed st 8 sts.
Work 8 (9: 9: 10: 10) rows, working one extra st in seed st on every row as set by last 4 rows (16 (17: 17: 18: 18) sts now in seed st).
Work a further 11 (10: 10: 11: 11) rows but now working one extra st in seed st on 3rd and every foll 3rd row, ending with a RS row (19 (20: 20: 21: 21) sts now in seed st).

Shape shoulder
Bind off 8 sts at beg of next and foll alt row, then 7 (7: 8: 8: 9) sts at beg of foll alt row, ending with a WS row.
Do NOT break yarn but leave rem 19 (20: 20: 21: 21) sts on a holder and set aside this ball of yarn.

SLEEVES (both alike)
Cast on 59 (59: 61: 63: 63) sts using size 3 (3.25mm) needles and yarn A.
Beg with a K row, work in St st for 10 rows, ending with a WS row.
Cont in patt as foll:
Row 1 (RS): K5 (5: 6: 7: 7), *P1, K7, rep from * to last 6 (6: 7: 8: 8) sts, P1, K5 (5: 6: 7: 7).
Working all increases in same way as for back and fronts and beg with a P row, work in St st for 9 rows, inc 1 st at each end of 4th of these rows. *61 (61: 63: 65: 65) sts.*
Row 11 (RS): K2 (2: 3: 4: 4), *P1, K7, rep from * to last 3 (3: 4: 5: 5) sts, P1, K2 (2: 3: 4: 4).
Beg with a P row, work in St st for 9 rows, inc 1 st at each end of 0 (8th: 8th: 8th: 6th) of these rows. *61 (63: 65: 67: 67) sts.*
Last 20 rows form patt and start sleeve shaping.
Cont in patt, shaping sides by inc 1 st at each end of next (11th: 13th: 13th: 9th) and every foll 14th (12th: 12th: 12th: 12th) row to 73 (75: 77: 79: 73) sts, then on every foll - (-: -: -: 10th) row until there are - (-: -: -: 81) sts, taking inc sts into patt.
Cont even until sleeve measures 14 (14: 14$^1/_2$: 14$^1/_2$: 14$^1/_2$)in/36 (36: 37: 37: 37)cm, ending with a WS row.

Shape top
Keeping patt correct, bind off 3 (4: 4: 5: 5) sts at beg of next 2 rows. *67 (67: 69: 69: 71) sts.*
Dec 1 st at each end of next 5 rows, then on foll 2 alt rows, then on every foll 4th row until 41 (41: 43: 43: 45) sts rem.
Work 1 row, ending with a WS row.
Dec 1 st at each end of next and every foll alt row to 35 sts, then on foll row, ending with a WS row. *33 sts.*
Bind off 4 sts at beg of next 2 rows.
Bind off rem 25 sts.

FINISHING
PRESS as described on the information page 138.
Join both shoulder seams using back stitch, or
mattress stitch if preferred.

Collar
With RS facing, using size 2 (3mm) needles and
ball of yarn A set to one side with right front, seed
st across 19 (20: 20: 21: 21) sts of right front, pick
up and knit 31 (33: 33: 35: 35) sts from back, then
seed st across 19 (20: 20: 21: 21) sts of left front.
69 (73: 73: 77: 77) sts.
Work in seed st as set by fronts for 1¼in/3cm.
Bind off in seed st.

Cuffs (both alike)
Cast on 63 (63: 65: 67: 67) sts using size 2 (3mm)
needles and yarn A.
Work in seed st as given for back for 3in/8cm.
Bind off in seed st.
See information page 138 for finishing
instructions, setting in sleeves using the set-
in method. Join row-end edges of cuffs for
1¼in/3cm from bound-off edge. Positioning cuff
seam directly opposite sleeve seam, sew bound-
off edge of cuffs to lower edges of sleeves. Fold
cuffs to RS. Using yarn B, embroider a French
knot (see tip page 128) onto each P st of pattern
on upper sections of back, fronts, and sleeves.

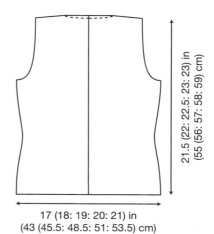

21.5 (22: 22.5: 23: 23) in
(55 (56: 57: 58: 59) cm)

17 (18: 19: 20: 21) in
(43 (45.5: 48.5: 51: 53.5) cm)

14 (14: 14.5: 14.5: 14.5) in
(36 (36: 37: 37: 37) cm)

Harriet

This very elegant fitted sweater comes in two different guises, one with a frilled edge to the polo neck, cuffs, and welt and the other with a simpler ribbed design. It was originally knitted in Rowan *4ply Soft* but Rowan *Cashsoft 4ply* makes an excellent substitute for the original yarn. *Cashsoft* has a wide color palette, and the dark gray Thunder or the light gray Weather are good alternatives, but any of the deep tones, like a deep burgundy (Redwood 429), navy (Deep 431), or purple (Loganberry 430), would look great.

YARN AND SIZES

To fit bust	XS	S	M	L	XL	
	32	34	36	38	40	in
	81	86	91	97	102	cm

4ply (CYCA Light) yarn
Rowan *Cashsoft 4ply* (57% fine merino wool, 33% microfiber, 10% cashmere; 197yd/50g)
Sweater with ribs in Weather 425

8	8	9	9	10	balls

(Originally photographed in Rowan *4ply Soft* in Sooty 372)

Sweater with frills in Thunder 437 and Weather 425

9	9	10	10	11	balls

(Originally photographed in Rowan *4ply Soft* in Sooty 372 and Whisper 370)

NEEDLES
1 pair size 2 (3mm) needles
1 pair size 3 (3.25mm) needles
Sweater with frills only: size 2 (3mm) circular needle

GAUGE
28 sts and 36 rows to 4in/10cm measured over stockinette stitch using size 3 (3.25mm) needles *or size necessary to obtain correct gauge*.

YARN NOTE
This garment was knitted originally in Rowan *4ply Soft*. We suggest you substitute Rowan *Cashsoft 4ply,* which knits to a very similar gauge. However, make sure you do a gauge swatch and, if necessary, adapt your needle size (up or down) to achieve the gauge on the pattern. If you do not, even a couple of stitches/rows difference on a thick yarn over a 4in/10cm swatch will make a noticeable difference to the width/length of the garment. For further information, see page 140.

Sweater with ribs

BACK

Cast on 114 (120: 128: 134: 142) sts using size 2 (3mm) needles.

Row 1 (RS): P0 (2: 0: 2: 0), K3 (4: 3: 4: 3), *P3, K4, rep from * to last 6 (2: 6: 2: 6) sts, P3 (2: 3: 2: 3), K3 (0: 3: 0: 3).

Row 2: K0 (2: 0: 2: 0), P3 (4: 3: 4: 3), *K3, P4, rep from * to last 6 (2: 6: 2: 6) sts, K3 (2: 3: 2: 3), P3 (0: 3: 0: 3).

These 2 rows form rib.

Work in rib for a further 4 rows, ending with a WS row.

Change to size 3 (3.25mm) needles.

Cont in rib, shaping side seams by dec 1 st at each end of 3rd and every foll 4th row until 102 (108: 116: 122: 130) sts rem.

Work 1 row, ending with a WS row.

Change to size 2 (3mm) needles.

Work 2 rows.

Dec 1 st at each end of next row.

100 (106: 114: 120: 128) sts rem.

Work 13 rows, ending with a WS row.

Change to size 3 (3.25mm) needles.

Inc 1 st at each end of next and every foll 8th row until there are 106 (112: 120: 126: 134) sts, taking inc sts into rib.

Work a further 7 rows, ending with a WS row. (70 rows of rib completed.)

Next row (RS): K2, M1, K to last 2 sts, M1, K2. *108 (114: 122: 128: 136) sts.*

Working all increases as set by last row and beg with a P row, cont in St st, shaping side seams by inc 1 st at each end of every foll 8th row until there are 114 (120: 128: 134: 142) sts.

Cont even until back measures 12 (12$\frac{1}{4}$: 12$\frac{1}{4}$: 12$\frac{1}{2}$: 12$\frac{1}{2}$)in/30 (31: 31: 32: 32)cm, ending with a WS row.

Shape armholes

Bind off 5 (6: 6: 7: 7) sts at beg of next 2 rows. *104 (108: 116: 120: 128) sts.*

Dec 1 st at each end of next 5 (5: 7: 7: 9) rows, then on foll 4 (5: 5: 6: 6) alt rows. *86 (88: 92: 94: 98) sts.*

Cont even until armhole measures 8 (8: 8$\frac{1}{4}$: 8$\frac{1}{4}$: 8$\frac{3}{4}$)in/20 (20: 21: 21: 22)cm, ending with a WS row.

Shape shoulders and back neck

Bind off 6 (6: 7: 7: 8) sts at beg of next 2 rows. *74 (76: 78: 80: 82) sts.*

Next row (RS): Bind off 6 (6: 7: 7: 8) sts, K until there are 11 sts on right needle and turn, leaving rem sts on a holder.

Work each side of neck separately.

Bind off 4 sts at beg of next row.

Bind off rem 7 sts.

With RS facing, rejoin yarn to rem sts, bind off

center 40 (42: 42: 44: 44) sts, K to end.
Complete to match first side, reversing shapings.

FRONT
Work as given for back until 24 (24: 24: 26: 26) rows less have been worked than on back to start of shoulder shaping, ending with a WS row.
Shape neck
Next row (RS): K32 (32: 34: 35: 37) and turn, leaving rem sts on a holder.
Work each side of neck separately.
Dec 1 st at neck edge of next 8 rows, then on foll 4 (4: 4: 5: 5) alt rows, then on foll 4th row.
19 (19: 21: 21: 23) sts.
Work 3 rows, ending with a WS row.
Shape shoulder
Bind off 6 (6: 7: 7: 8) sts at beg of next and foll alt row.
Work 1 row.
Bind off rem 7 sts.
With RS facing, rejoin yarn to rem sts, bind off center 22 (24: 24: 24: 24) sts, K to end.
Complete to match first side, reversing shapings.

SLEEVES (both alike)
Cast on 57 (57: 59: 61: 61) sts using size 2 (3mm) needles.
Row 1 (RS): P2 (2: 0: 0: 0), K4 (4: 0: 1: 1), *P3, K4, rep from * to last 2 (2: 3: 4: 4) sts, P2 (2: 3: 3: 3), K0 (0: 0: 1: 1).
Row 2: K2 (2: 0: 0: 0), P4 (4: 0: 1: 1), *K3, P4, rep from * to last 2 (2: 3: 4: 4) sts, K2 (2: 3: 3: 3), P0 (0: 0: 1: 1).
These 2 rows form rib.
Work in rib for a further 8 rows, ending with a WS row.
Change to size 3 (3.25mm) needles.
Cont in rib, shaping sides by inc 1 st at each end of 9th and every foll 10th row until there are 69 (69: 71: 73: 73) sts, taking inc sts into rib.

Work 1 row, ending with a WS row. (70 rows of rib completed.) Working all increases as set by side seam incs and beg with a K row, cont in St st, shaping sides by inc 1 st at each end of 7th and every foll 8th row to 75 (75: 77: 79: 79) sts, then on every foll 6th row to 81 (77: 83: 85: 81) sts, then on every foll 4th row until there are 95 (97: 99: 101: 103) sts.
Cont even until sleeve measures 17 (17: 17$\frac{1}{2}$: 17$\frac{1}{2}$: 17$\frac{1}{2}$)in/43 (43: 44: 44: 44)cm, ending with a WS row.
Shape top
Bind off 5 (6: 6: 7: 7) sts at beg of next 2 rows.
85 (85: 87: 87: 89) sts.
Dec 1 st at each end of next 5 rows, then on foll 3 alt rows, then on every foll 4th row until 57 (57: 59: 59: 61) sts rem.
Work 1 row, ending with a WS row.
Dec 1 st at each end of next and every foll alt row until 49 sts rem, then on foll 5 rows, ending with a WS row.
Bind off rem 39 sts.

Sweater with frills
BACK
Cast on 429 (453: 485: 509: 541) sts using size 2 (3mm) circular needle.
Row 1 (RS): K1, *K2, lift first of these 2 sts over second st and off right needle, rep from * to end.
Row 2: P1, *P2tog, rep from * to end.
108 (114: 122: 128: 136) sts.
These 2 rows complete frill edging.
Change to size 3 (3.25mm) needles.
Beg with a K row, work in St st for 20 rows, ending with a WS row.
Counting in from both ends of last row, place markers on 25th (27th: 30th: 32nd: 35th) st in from row ends.
Row 21 (RS): K2, K2tog, [K to within 2 sts of marked st, K2tog tbl, K marked st, K2tog] twice, K

to last 4 sts, K2tog tbl, K2.
102 (108: 116: 122: 130) sts.
Work 5 rows.
Row 27 (RS): [K to within 2 sts of marked st, K2tog tbl, K marked st, K2tog] twice, K to end.
98 (104: 112: 118: 126) sts.
Work 5 rows.
Row 33: As row 21. *92 (98: 106: 112: 120) sts.*
Work 13 rows.
Row 47 (RS): K2, M1, [K to marked st, M1, K marked st, M1] twice, K to last 2 sts, M1, K2.
98 (104: 112: 118: 126) sts.
Work 9 rows.
Rep last 10 rows twice more.
110 (116: 124: 130: 138) sts.
Working side seam inc as set, inc 1 st at each end of next and foll 10th row.
114 (120: 128: 134: 142) sts.
Cont even until back measures 12 (12¼: 12¼: 12½: 12½)in/30 (31: 31: 32: 32)cm from top of frill, ending with a WS row.
Shape armholes
Bind off 5 (6: 6: 7: 7) sts at beg of next 2 rows.
104 (108: 116: 120: 128) sts.
Dec 1 st at each end of next 5 (5: 7: 7: 9) rows, then on foll 4 (5: 5: 6: 6) alt rows.
86 (88: 92: 94: 98) sts.
Cont even until armhole measures 8 (8: 8¼: 8¼: 8¾)in/20 (20: 21: 21: 22)cm, ending with a WS row.
Shape shoulders and back neck
Bind off 8 (8: 8: 8: 9) sts at beg of next 2 rows.
70 (72: 76: 78: 80) sts.
Next row (RS): Bind off 8 (8: 8: 8: 9) sts, K until there are 11 (11: 13: 13: 13) sts on right needle and turn, leaving rem sts on a holder.
Work each side of neck separately.
Bind off 4 sts at beg of next row.
Bind off rem 7 (7: 9: 9: 9) sts.
With RS facing, rejoin yarn to rem sts, bind off center 32 (34: 34: 36: 36) sts, K to end.
Complete to match first side, reversing shapings.

FRONT

Work as given for back until 24 (24: 24: 26: 26) rows fewer have been worked than on back to start of shoulder shaping, ending with a WS row.
Shape neck
Next row (RS): K36 (36: 38: 39: 41) and turn, leaving rem sts on a holder.
Work each side of neck separately.
Bind off 4 sts at beg of next row.
32 (32: 34: 35: 37) sts.
Dec 1 st at neck edge of next 5 rows, then on foll 2 (2: 2: 3: 3) alt rows, then on every foll 4th row until 23 (23: 25: 25: 27) sts rem.
Work 5 rows, ending with a WS row.
Shape shoulder
Bind off 8 (8: 8: 8: 9) sts at beg of next and foll alt row.
Work 1 row.
Bind off rem 7 (7: 9: 9: 9) sts.
With RS facing, rejoin yarn to rem sts, bind off center 14 (16: 16: 16: 16) sts, K to end.
Complete to match first side, reversing shapings.

SLEEVES (both alike)

Cast on 225 (225: 233: 241: 241) sts using size 2 (3mm) circular needle.
Row 1 (RS): K1, *K2, lift first of these 2 sts over second st and off right needle, rep from * to end.
Row 2: P1, *P2tog, rep from * to end.
57 (57: 59: 61: 61) sts.
These 2 rows complete frill edging.
Change to size 3 (3.25mm) needles.
Beg with a K row, work in St st, shaping sides by inc 1 st at each end of 19th and every foll 10th row to 69 (69: 71: 73: 73) sts, then on every foll 8th row to 75 (75: 77: 79: 79) sts, then on every foll 6th row to 81 (77: 83: 85: 81) sts, then on every foll 4th row

until there are 95 (97: 99: 101: 103) sts.
Cont even until sleeve measures 17 (17: 17$\frac{1}{2}$: 17$\frac{1}{2}$: 17$\frac{1}{2}$)in/43 (43: 44: 44: 44)cm from top of frill, ending with a WS row.

Shape top

Bind off 5 (6: 6: 7: 7) sts at beg of next 2 rows. *85 (85: 87: 87: 89) sts.*

Dec 1 st at each end of next 5 rows, then on foll 5 (5: 6: 6: 7) alt rows, then on every foll 4th row to 49 sts, then on every foll 5th row until 41 sts rem. Work 3 rows, ending with a WS row.
Bind off rem 41 sts.

FINISHING

PRESS as described on the information page 138. Join right shoulder seam using back stitch, or mattress stitch if preferred.

Sweater with ribs only
Neckband

With RS facing and using size 2 (3mm) needles, pick up and knit 24 (24: 24: 26: 26) sts down left side of neck, 22 (24: 24: 24: 24) sts from front, 24 (24: 24: 26: 26) sts up right side of neck, then 48 (50: 50: 52: 52) sts from back.
118 (122: 122: 128: 128) sts.

Beg with a K row, work in rev St st for 5 rows.
Bind off loosely.
See information page 138 for finishing instructions, setting in sleeves using the set-in method.

Sweater with frills only
Collar

With RS facing and using size 2 (3mm) needles, pick up and knit 30 (30: 32: 33: 33) sts down left side of neck, 14 (16: 16: 16: 16) sts from front, 30 (30: 32: 33: 33) sts up right side of neck, then 40 (42: 42: 44: 44) sts from back. *114 (118: 122: 126: 126) sts.*

Row 1 (WS): P2, *K2, P2, rep from * to end.
Row 2: K2, *P2, K2, rep from * to end.

Rep these 2 rows for 3in/8cm, ending with a WS row.
Change to size 2 (3mm) circular needle.
Next row (RS): *K1, M1, rep from * to last st, K1.
Next row: *P1, M1 purlwise, rep from * to last st, P1. *453 (469: 485: 501: 501) sts.*
Bind off loosely.
See information page 138 for finishing instructions, setting in sleeves using the puffed sleeve method and gathering top of sleeve to fit armhole.

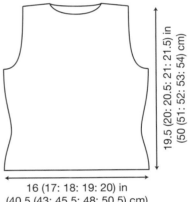

16 (17: 18: 19: 20) in
(40.5 (43: 45.5: 48: 50.5) cm)

19.5 (20: 20.5: 21: 21.5) in
(50 (51: 52: 53: 54) cm)

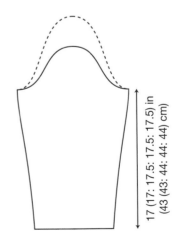

17 (17: 17.5: 17.5: 17.5) in
(43 (43: 44: 44: 44) cm)

Useful information

GAUGE

Obtaining the correct gauge is perhaps the single factor which can make the difference between a successful garment and a disastrous one. It controls both the shape and size of an article, so any variation, however slight, can distort the finished garment. We recommend that you knit a square in pattern and/or stockinette stitch (depending on the pattern instructions) with perhaps 5–10 more stitches and 5–10 more rows than those given in the gauge note. Mark out the central 4in/10cm square with pins. If you have too many stitches to 4in/10cm, try again using thicker needles; if you have too few stitches to 4in/10cm, try again using finer needles. Once you have achieved the correct gauge your garment will be knitted to the measurements indicated in the size diagram shown at the end of the pattern.

SIZING AND SIZE DIAGRAM NOTE

The instructions are given for the smallest size. Where they vary, work the figures in brackets for the larger sizes. One set of figures refers to all sizes. Included with most patterns is a "size diagram" or sketch of the finished garment and its dimensions. The size diagram shows the finished width of the garment at the under-arm point, and it is this measurement that the knitter should go by when working out the right size; a useful tip is to measure one of your own garments which is a comfortable fit. Having chosen a size based on width, look at the corresponding length for that size; if you are not happy with the total length which we recommend, adjust your own garment before beginning your armhole shaping—any adjustment after this point will mean that your sleeve will not fit into your garment easily—don't forget to take your adjustment into account if there is any side seam shaping. Finally, look at the sleeve length; the size diagram shows the finished sleeve measurement, taking into account any top-arm insertion length. Measure your body between the center of your neck and your wrist, this measurement should correspond to half the garment width plus the sleeve length. Again, your sleeve length may be adjusted, but remember

to take into consideration your sleeve increases if you do adjust the length—you must increase more frequently than the pattern states to shorten your sleeve, less frequently to lengthen it.

FINISHING INSTRUCTIONS

It can take many hours to knit a garment, so it seems a great pity that many garments are spoiled because such little care is taken in the pressing and finishing process. The following tips offer a truly professional-looking garment.

PRESSING

Pin out each piece of knitting on a board (known as blocking) and, following the instructions on the ball band, press the garment pieces, omitting the ribs (**note:** take special care to press the edges, as this will make sewing up both easier and neater). If the ball band indicates that the fabric is not to be pressed, then covering the blocked-out fabric with a damp white cotton cloth and leaving it to stand will have the desired effect. Darn in all ends neatly along the selvedge edge or a color join, as appropriate.

STITCHING

When stitching the pieces together, match areas of color and texture very carefully where they meet. Use back stitch or mattress stitch for all main knitting seams and join all ribs and neckband with mattress stitch, unless otherwise stated.

CONSTRUCTION

Having completed the pattern instructions, join left shoulder and neckband seams as detailed above. Sew the top of the sleeve to the body of the garment using the method detailed in the pattern, referring to the appropriate guide:
Shallow set-in sleeves: Match decreases at beginning of armhole shaping to decreases at top of sleeve. Sew sleeve head into armhole, easing in shapings.
Set-in sleeves: Place center of bound-off edge of sleeve to shoulder seam. Set in sleeve, easing sleeve head into armhole. Join side and sleeve seams. Slip stitch pocket edgings and linings into place. Sew

on buttons to correspond with buttonholes. Ribbed welts and neckbands and any areas of garter stitch should not be pressed.

Puffed set-in sleeves: Run a row of gathering stitches around the top part of the sleeve head and make a knot at the end of the thread. With right sides facing, pin the top of the sleeve head to the shoulder seam of the garment. Gently pull the ends of the gathering thread until the sleeve head fits the size of the armhole and then pin and baste into position before stitching in the usual way.

MEASURING GUIDE

For maximum comfort and to ensure the correct fit, follow the tips below when checking your size:

Measure yourself close to your body, over your underwear. Don't pull the tape measure too tight!

Bust/chest—measure around the fullest part of the bust/chest and across the shoulder blades.

Waist—measure around the natural waistline, just above the hip bone.

Hips—measure around the fullest part of the bottom.

If you don't wish to measure yourself, measure the size of a favorite sweater that you like the fit of and compare these measurements with the size diagram given at the end of the individual instructions.

GAUGE NOTE: Remember, if your gauge is too loose, your garment will be bigger than the pattern size and you may use more yarn. If your gauge is too tight, your garment could be smaller than the pattern size and you will have yarn left over. Always check your gauge before starting a project.

NEEDLE SIZE NOTE: Kim's designs originate in the UK, where metric needle sizes are used. As some US needle sizes do not equate precisely to metric needle sizes, we have given the US needle size that will reflects Kim's original design.

ABBREVIATIONS

alt	alternate	**mm**	millimeters		stitches decreased
approx	approximately	**oz**	ounce(s)	**sl1**	slip one stitch
beg	begin(ning)	**patt**	pattern	**sl st(s)**	slip stitch(es)
cont	continue	**P**	purl	**st(s)**	stitch(es)
cm	centimeters	**P2tog**	purl two stitches together	**St st**	stockinette stitch (1 row K, 1 row P)
dec	decreas(e)(ing)				
foll	follow(ing)(s)	**psso**	pass slipped stitch over	**tbl**	through back of loop(s)
garter st	garter stitch (K every row)	**0**	no stitches, times or rows for that size	**tog**	together
				WS	wrong side
g	gram(s)	**rem**	remain(ing)	**yd**	yard
in	inch(es)	**rep**	repeat	**yo**	yarn over
inc	increas(e)(ing)	**RS**	right side	*	repeat all instructions between asterisks
K	knit	**rev St st**	reverse stockinette stitch (1 row P, 1 row K)		
K2tog	knit two stitches together			[ ]	repeat instructions between square brackets as indicated
		skp	slip, knit, pass stitch over; one stitch decreased		
M1	make one stitch by picking up horizontal loop before next stitch and knitting back of it				
		sk2p	slip 1, knit 2 together, pass slip stitch over the K2tog stitch; two		
m	meter				

Substituting yarns

Rowan Yarns has always been a fashion-led brand, and over the years their yarns and colors have changed to reflect trends. So when choosing patterns from the Rowan magazines for this book, we found that some of the older designs used yarns that were no longer in production, or the yarn was still available but the colors weren't. For these designs, substitute yarns and/or new colors were selected. The replacement yarns and colors echo as closely as possible the originals.

Substituting yarns is not always straightforward and much testing and re-testing went into our new yarn choices. If you want to try to substitute yarns yourself, read the guidelines that follow and be aware that some patterns may prove difficult to find substitutes for, either because the original colors are hard to match or because a particular yarn or stitch pattern make the task harder than usual.

Substituting a standard-weight yarn

The easiest yarns to find substitutes for are ordinary smooth yarns in one of the standard weights—for example, UK 4ply, double-knitting and Aran weights, and US sport and worsted weights. But even a standard-weight wool yarn won't necessarily have the exact same thickness (or diameter) as another yarn in the same category. This is because yarns have different loft—air between the fibers—and springiness. So a standard yarn weight is not determined by its diameter but by ideal gauge measured over stockinette stitch using a specific needle size.

Even though yarn manufacturers attempt to match the recognized standard gauges for their standard-weight yarns, these are not always precisely the same from brand to brand. Before purchasing a substitute for a standard-weight yarn, check the yarn label and see if it matches the recommended gauge and needle size of the original yarn. The specifications for the yarns used in this book are listed on pages 142–143 for this purpose.

If gauge and needle size match exactly, you have probably found a good substitute. If the stitch gauge is the same but the row gauge is slightly different, you may still be able to use it as your substitute as long as your garment has a simple shape without shaped sleeve tops and the pattern tells you to knit to a certain measurement rather than a certain number of rows.

Choosing a matching yarn texture

Finding substitutes for non-standard-weight yarns or yarns in anything other than ordinary smooth wool yarns is a little more difficult, but it follows the same principle: look for a yarn with the same recommended gauge and needle size.

Aside from yarn weight, you must also try to match the original yarn's fiber content and texture. Using a yarn with a totally different fiber content is unlikely to give you a garment that looks like the original. It won't have either the same drape or the same firmness. So, for example, if the original yarn is a cotton, look for a cotton replacement. Choosing a substitute for a mohair yarn illustrates this point very clearly. If you choose anything other than another mohair yarn, the result will be vastly different from the original design.

Testing your substitute yarn

Once you've found what you think will be a good substitute yarn, it is essential to knit a gauge swatch to test its suitability, even if you are substituting a smooth, standard-weight yarn. Buy just one ball for this purpose and only buy all the balls you need once you have tested your substitute.

Knit as many swatches as you need to until you achieve the correct gauge with your replacement yarn, following the instructions on page 138. (If you can't achieve the correct gauge, you'll need to look for another substitute.)

Having achieved a gauge that matches the one specified in the pattern, study your swatch carefully. Does it feel nice? Does it look like the fabric in the photograph? If your swatch is floppy but the garment looks structured, try another, firmer yarn or one that is very slightly thicker. You may need to try a few substitutes before you find one that gives you just the right feel and look.

Choosing substitute colors

A substitute yarn may not come in the same shade as the one-color original design, but most yarns have a good selection of colors for you to choose from. Multicolored designs are more difficult to find good matches for, so keep this in mind when choosing a replacement yarn. If the shade range is too limited, you may need to look for an alternative or create a new colorway.

When creating a colorway (or trying to find colors that match the originals), bear in mind the depth and tone of each of the original shades. Check the original photograph. Does one color "jump out" at you? If so, then choose your new colors so that this shade will still "jump out." Or do all the colors subtly harmonize with each other? In which case, your substitute colors must harmonize as well.

Take into account the lightness and darkness of the various shades in the design as much as the actual hue of the color. The less contrast there is between the various tones, the more subtle and soft the colorway, and the higher the contrast the bolder the effect.

The best way to choose your replacement colors is to arrange the different colored balls of yarn roughly in the order they appear in the design. Holding single strands together isn't as helpful and won't give you a feel for the type of effect the shades will create. Then test your choices with a swatch. Press your swatch, and pin it up on a board so you can check it from a distance, as well as close up, before deciding on your final colors.

Purchasing the right amount of yarn

Once you are ready to purchase all the yarn needed for your garment, calculate how many yards you need. Don't try to determine yarn amounts by ball weight, as yarns, even of those in the same weight category, vary in weight per yard.

Successful yarn substitutions

Armed with the basics for yarn substitution, you're ready to go out and "play" with different yarns and colors. Whatever you do, just remember you must match the gauge in the pattern instructions and, ideally, you should aim for a knitted fabric of a similar weight and firmness or drape. Beyond that, the only limitation is your imagination and creativity.

Yarn information

The following yarns are those specified in the patterns in this book. Rowan *Felted Tweed*, *Felted Tweed Aran*, and *Felted Tweed Chunky* have replaced Rowan *Scottish Tweed DK*, *Aran*, and *Chunky* used in some of the original patterns. Rowan *Cashsoft 4ply* replaces Rowan *4ply Soft* used in one original pattern. When using substitute yarns, always take care to check your gauge carefully by knitting a preliminary gauge square and by altering knitting needle sizes as necessary to obtain the specified gauge in the pattern (see page 138). Failure to obtain the correct gauge will affect the fit/size of the relevant garment.

Rowan *All Seasons Cotton*
Worsted (CYCA Light) yarn
60 percent cotton, 40 percent acrylic/microfiber; 1¾oz/50g (approx 98yd/90m) per ball. Recommended gauge: 16–18 sts and 23–25 rows to 4in/10cm measured over St st using size 7–9 (4.5–5.5mm) knitting needles.

Rowan *British Sheep Breeds DK*
DK (CYCA Light) yarn
100 percent British wool; 1¾oz/50g (approx 131yd/120m) per ball. Recommended gauge: 22 sts and 30 rows to 4in/10cm measured over St st using size 6 (4mm) knitting needles.

Rowan *Calmer*
Aran (CYCA Medium) yarn
75 percent cotton, 25 percent acrylic microfiber; 1¾oz/50g (approx 175yd/160m) per ball. Recommended gauge: 21 sts and 30 rows to 4in/10cm measured over St st using size 8 (5mm) knitting needles.

Rowan *Cashsoft 4ply*
4ply (CYCA Fine) yarn
57 percent fine merino wool, 33 percent microfiber, 10 percent cashmere; 1¾oz/50g (approx197yd/180m) per ball. Recommended gauge: 28 sts and 36 rows to 4in/10cm measured over St st using size 3 (3.25mm) knitting needles.

Rowan *Cocoon*
Aran (CYCA Medium) yarn
80 percent merino wool/20 percent kid mohair yarn; 3½oz/100g (approx 226yd/115m) per ball. Recommended gauge: 14 sts and 16 rows to 4in/10cm measured over St st using size 10½ (7mm) knitting needles.

Rowan *Cotton Glace*
DK (CYCA Light) yarn
100 percent cotton yarn; 1¾oz/50g (approx 126yd/115m) per ball. Recommended gauge: 23 sts and 32 rows to 4in/10cm measured over St st using size 3–5 (3.25–3.75mm) knitting needles.

Rowan *Denim*
Worsted (CYCA Medium) yarn
100 percent cotton yarn; 1¾oz/50g (approx 102yd/93m) per ball. Recommended gauge: 20sts and 28 rows to 4in/10cm measured over St st using size 6 (4mm) knitting needles.

Rowan *Felted Tweed*
DK (CYCA Light) yarn
50 percent merino wool, 25 percent alpaca wool, 25 percent viscose; 1¾oz/50g (approx 191yd/175m) per ball. Recommended gauge: 22–24 sts and 30–32 rows to 4in/10cm measured over St st using size 5–6 (3.75–4mm) knitting needles.

Rowan *Felted Tweed Aran*
Aran (CYCA Medium) yarn
50 percent merino wool, 25 percent alpaca, 15 percent viscose; 1¾oz/50g (95yd/87m) per ball. Recommended gauge: 16sts and 23 rows to 4in/10cm measured over St st using size 8 (5mm) knitting needles.

Rowan *Fine Heritage Tweed*
Sport (CYCA Fine) yarn
100 percent wool yarn; ⁷⁄₈oz/25g (approx 98yd/90m) per ball. Recommended gauge: 26–27 sts and 38 rows to 4in/10cm measured over St st using size 3 (3.25mm) knitting needles.

Rowan *Heritage Tweed*
DK (CYCA Light) yarn
100 percent wool yarn; 1¾oz/50g (approx 129yd/118m) per ball. Recommended gauge: 21 sts and 30 rows to 4in/10cm measured over St st using size 6 (4mm) knitting needles.

Rowan *Kid Classic*
Worsted (CYCA Light) yarn
70 percent lambswool, 25 percent kid mohair, 4 percent nylon; 1¾oz/50g (153yd/140m) per ball. Recommended gauge: 18–19 sts and 23–25 rows to 4in/10cm measured over St st using size 8–9 (5–5.5mm) knitting needles.

Rowan *Kidsilk Haze*
Lightweight (CYCA Light) yarn
70 percent super kid mohair, 30 percent silk; ⁷⁄₈oz/25g (approx 229yd/210m) per ball. Recommended gauge: 18–25 sts and 23–34 rows to 4in/10cm measured over St st using size 3–8 (3.25–5mm) knitting needles.

Rowan *Siena*
4ply (CYCA Super Fine) yarn
100 percent mercerized cotton; 1¾oz/50g (approx 153yd/140m) per ball. Recommended gauge: 28 sts and 38 rows to 4in/10cm over St st using size 2–3 (2.75–3.25mm) knitting needles.

Rowan *Wool Cotton*
DK (CYCA Light) yarn
50 percent merino wool, 50 percent cotton; 1¾oz/50g (approx 123yd/113m) per ball. Recommended gauge: 22–24 sts and 30–32 rows to 4in/10cm measured over St st using size 5–6 (3.75–4mm) knitting needles.

Buying yarns

Rowan yarns (and buttons) have been used for all the knitting patterns in this book. See page opposite for descriptions of the yarns used. To find out where to buy Rowan yarns near you, contact one of the Rowan yarn distributors given below. The main Rowan office is in the United Kingdom (see below for their website). For stockists in all other countries please contact Rowan for details.

ROWAN YARN DISTRIBUTORS

U.S.A.: Westminster Fibers Inc, 8 Shelter Drive, Greer, 29650, South Carolina
Tel: (800) 445-9276
Email: info@westminsterfibers.com
Web: www.westminsterfibers.com

AUSTRALIA: Australian Country Spinners Pty Ltd, Level 7, 409 St. Kilda Road, Melbourne 3004.
Tel: 03 9380 3830
Email: tkohut@auspinners.com.au

AUSTRIA: Coats Harlander GmbH, Autokaderstrasse 31, Wien A -1210.
Tel: (01) 27716

BELGIUM: Coats Benelux, Ring Oost 14A, Ninove, 9400
Tel: 054 318989
Email: sales.coatsninove@coats.com

CANADA: Westminster Fibers, 8 Shelter Drive, Greer, South Carolina, 29650
Tel: 800 445-9276
Email: info@westminsterfibers.com
Web: www.westminsterfibers.com

CHINA: Coats Shanghai Ltd, No 9 Building , Baosheng Road, Songjiang Industrial Zone, Shanghai.
Tel: 86 21 5774 3733
Email: victor.li@coats.com

DENMARK: Coats HP A/S, Tagensvej 85C, St.tv., Copenhagen
Tel: 45 35 86 90 49

FINLAND: Coats Opti Crafts Oy, Ketjutie 3, Kerava , 04220
Tel: (358) 9 274871
Email: coatsopti@coats.com
Web: www.coatscrafts.fi

FRANCE: Coats Steiner, 100 Avenue du Général de Gaulle, Mehun-Sur-Yèvre, 18500
Tel: 02 48 23 12 30
Web: www.coatscrafts.fr

GERMANY: Coats GmbH, Kaiserstrasse 1, Kenzingen, 79341
Tel: 07162-14346
Web: www.coatsgmbh.de

HOLLAND: Coats Benelux, Ring Oost 14A, Ninove, 9400, Belgium
Tel: 0346 35 37 00
Email: sales.coatsninove@coats.com

HONG KONG: Coats Shanghai Ltd, No 8 Building , Export & Processing Garden, Songjiang Industrial Zone, Shanghai, China.
Tel: (86- 21) 57743733-326
Email: victor.li@coats.com

ICELAND: Rowan At Storkurinn, Laugavegur 59, Reykjavik, 101
Tel: 551 8258
Email: storkurinn@simnet.is
Web: www.storkurinn.is

ISRAEL: Beit Hasidkit, Ms. Offra Tzenger, Sokolov St No 2, Kfar Sava, 44256
Tel: (972) 9 7482381

ITALY: Coats Cucirini srl, Viale Sarca 223, Milano, 20126
Tel: 02 636151
Web: www.coatscucirini.com

KOREA: Coats Korea Co. Lt, 5F Eyeon B/D, 935-40 Bangbae-Dong, Seocho-Gu, Seoul, 137-060
Tel: 82-2-521-6262
Web: www.coatskorea.co.kr

LEBANON: y.knot, Saifi Village, Mkhalissiya Street 162, Beirut
Tel: (961) 1 992211
Email: y.knot@cyberia.net.lb

LUXEMBOURG: Coats Benelux, Ring Oost 14A, Ninove, 9400, Belgium
Tel: 0346 35 37 00
Email: sales.coatsninove@coats.com

MALTA: John Gregory Ltd, 8 Ta'Xbiex Sea Front, Msida, MSD 1512, Malta
Tel: +356 2133 0202
Email: raygreg@onvol.net

NEW ZEALAND: ACS New Zealand, 1 March Place, Belfast, Christchurch
Tel: 64-3-323-6665

NORWAY: Coats Knappehuset AS, Pb 100, Ulset, Bergen, 5873
Tel: 55 53 93 00

PORTUGAL: Coats & Clark, Quinta de Cravel, Apartado 444, Vila Nova de Gaia 4431-968
Tel: 223770700
Web: www.crafts.com.pt

SINGAPORE: Golden Dragon Store, 101 Upper Cross Street, #02-51, People's Park Center, 058357, Singapore
Tel: (65) 65358454/65358234
Email: gdscraft@hotmail.com

SOUTH AFRICA: Arthur Bales Ltd, 62 Fourth Avenue, Linden, Johannesburg, 2195
Tel: (27) 118 882 401
Email: arthurb@new.co.za
Web: www.arthurbales.co.za

SPAIN: Coats Fabra, SA, Santa Adria, 20, Barcelona, 08030
Tel: (34) 93 290 84 00
Email: atencion.clientes@coats.com
Web: www.coatscrafts.es

SWEDEN: Coats Expotex AB, JA Wettergrensgata 7, Vastra Frolunda, Goteborg, 431 30
Tel: (46) 33 720 79 00

SWITZERLAND: Coats Stroppel AG, Turgi (AG), CH-5300
Tel: 056 298 12 20

TAIWAN: Cactus Quality Co Ltd, 7FL-2, No. 140, Sec. 2 Roosevelt Road, Taipei, Taiwan, R.O.C. 10084
Tel: 00886-2-23656527
Email:cqcl@ms17.hinet.net
Web: www.excelcraft.com.tw

THAILAND: Global Wide Trading, 10 Lad Prao Soi 88, Bangkok 10310
Tel: 00 662 933 9019
Email: TheNeedleWorld@yahoo.com, global.wide@yahoo.com

U.K.: Rowan, Green Lane Mill, Holmfirth, West Yorkshire, England HD9 2DX
Tel: +44 (0) 1484 681881
Email: mail@knitrowan.com
Web: www.knitrowan.com